Published by Digitopia Studios Ltd.

ISBN 978-0-9927340-2-2

Written by Farhan Qureshi www.digitopiaDigital.com

Editorial and Page Layout by Vicki Watson www.callistogreen.com

Cover Design by Alex Mathers alexmathers.net

Start here…

This book is for you.

Yes, you. You the blogger.

This book isn't about how to craft the perfect blog post that nobody will ever read. This book isn't about spending hours looking for plugins that you will never use. This book is of use and you will gain real, tangible benefits from reading it. Not only that, but reading this book will allow you to take actionable steps that will make a real difference to your blog and your life as a blogger.

This book is entirely, 100% for you, you the blogger or the blogger-to-be.

Everything in this book is for bloggers by bloggers.

Introduction

Blogging is power

If you believe that knowledge is power then what you are holding in your hand right now is the 'Power Book of the Twenty First Century'.

A little overstated?

Perhaps.

But actually you already know that your blog is a powerful asset that you own, so why would you be blogging (or starting to blog) in the first place, if not to share your expertise and get your message across? Your blog is a powerful forum, and you created it yourself.

Two questions:

- How powerful is your blog?
- How powerful could it become?

That is what this book is all about. It's about giving you the ability to know exactly how much influence your blog has and what you could grow it to be. This book will help you go way beyond knowing just how many pageviews you have, where your visitors come from, how long they spend on your site and all those vanilla, top-level headline metrics.

What this book will give you is the ability to really understand why people come to your blog and how you can have them continue to return and attract more of the kind of visitors that you want.

What you are reading now is a structured course in exactly how you can do that, covering every facet from how to install a web analytics programme to how to track the effectiveness and engagement of promotional materials.

Want to know how much value this book holds for you?

Let's compare.

To attend a course that *covers part of the content that I am presenting* would set you back between £1,499 and £2,500 (that's $2,438 to $4,072). Not only are those courses about a hundred times more expensive than this book, but **this book is written for you – you the blogger.** The courses out there are general courses on Google Analytics or on ad serving, they'll walk you through the software (at about a hundred times the cost), but they're not built for bloggers.

There is actually a second audience for this book and that is as an unintended consequence of writing such a thorough and accessible text. I've been told again and again by people that they have managed to get themselves a job as a web analyst or an ad operation role based solely on putting into practice the techniques that I present in this book (though I do feel *'Essential Web Analytics for Bloggers'* is a more catchy title than *'Essential Web Analytics for Bloggers and Those Who Want To Get a Web Analytics and / or Ad Serving Job'*).

Whether it's the ebook or the paperback, what you are holding in your hands right now is something very powerful; it's the result of years of work, where I've been through the 'steep learning curve', hoping that this will bring you an immense amount of actionable benefits that you can immediately put into practice.

Who am I and why should you listen to me anyway?

Hello there. Thanks for picking up this book; clearly we have a lot in common.

We are both bloggers.

We both love blogging.

I'd venture to say that we may love blogging more than we love our day jobs.

I imagine we both share the same goal of wanting to earn money from our blogs and at some point make more money from our blogs than we do in our day jobs.

Sound about right?

There are many books and blogs about blogging. They talk about how to write the perfect blog post, they talk about how to get people to your site, how to capture their email addresses through a free ebook / whitepaper / newsletter sign-up form.

I've read them all too; some of them are very good. A lot though is just recycled material. Why recycle the same tips? Because it's easy to do so and puts that writer in a position of authority.

But what I haven't been able to find is a single book on analytics for bloggers. More precisely a book on how you can implement, analyse and action analytics in your blog.

Why are there no 'sign-up white papers' on this?

Because it's difficult and hugely time-consuming for these so-called 'blogging experts' to write one and there isn't one out there for them to copy. That's why I've written this book for you, because you won't find this material anywhere else.

Never mind understanding and acting on your analytics, even having access to your analytics will put you at a massive advantage over ninety-nine percent of the other bloggers out there. This book is going to give you both the insight and all the practical, step-by-step help you need to quickly identify the strongest parts of your blog and improve upon the weakest areas too.

So who exactly am I and why should you be reading this?

My name is Farhan, I live in London and I work as a head of analytics at a major publisher looking after the analytics of several of the world's market leading brands and blogs. I deal with a lot of analytics and use the treasures hidden away in them to develop blogging strategies that meet each brand's business goals.

For some it's generating traffic to increase banner advertising click through rates. For others it's lead generation, getting people to sign up for newsletters, having them complete surveys (and thereby capture valuable marketing data). And for others still it's pure ecommerce and shortening the cycle from intent to buy to actually making a purchase (and create ways for them to maximise the purchase).

Even more important than this and far more relevant to you is that much like you, I am a blogger too.

I currently run three blogs. One is an industry-leading filmmaking, VFX and animation blog, www.digitopiafilm.com, where I blog about filmmaking in the real world – before going into analytics I worked as a CGI artist for ten years (more details on the projects I worked on are here: http://www.imdb.com/name/nm1629604/).

When I was able to really understand the analytics, I was able to take this blog way beyond anywhere it had been before. I've used this blog to help source filmmaking and animation collaborators, develop storyboards, create an animation reference library, even to start crowdfunding projects – not to mention being able to target contextual advertising to the exact pages, ensuring the right advert is served to the right site visitor.

My second blog, www.workingParent.info, is a blog dedicated to parents who balance a full-time career/job hunting and parenthood. This is the first blog of its kind that actually focuses on the challenges that parents face when they spend more time at work than with their kids and how to maximise whatever time they do have with their children.

My third blog is called www.digitopiaDigital.com, a blog dedicated to helping you the blogger with all the digital tasks that will save you time and digital strategy that will help make your blog a success.

Using the analytics here, I can directly compare the different behaviours from these three contrasting audiences and know what works for each – yes, that's something else these blogging and analytics courses won't teach you, that each audience responds differently. What works for one may not work for the other. But don't worry this book will help you understand the unique traits of 'your audience' and help you give them what they want.

In all these cases I have implemented analytics into the blogs and in both cases I have managed to leverage the analytics in the blog to create revenue from my blogging.

Want to be able to do the same for your blog/blogs?

You've come to the right place. I'm going to walk you through the whole process, start to finish.

In Part One, we are going to talk about why you should even bother with all this hassle. Do you really have the time to be implementing all the analytics code in your blog? Wouldn't you be better off spending your time writing a blog post than deciphering JavaScript and trying to find the right place to put it? After reading Part One, you'll know why this is so important – and how easy and quick it is to do.

In Part Two, you'll find out how you can use your analytics to determine the difference between which metrics you think you ought to be focusing on versus which metrics you need to focus on. I'll show you how to sift through all the hundreds of metrics that your analytics software will throw at you and find those golden nuggets that you can use to start making money from your blog.

In the next three parts we'll get our hands dirty. I've divided the whole process into three distinct areas which I've called the three-step WAB (Web Analytics for Bloggers) formula.

Part Three shows you how to set up a Google Analytics account (you probably already have one but may not know about it), create a web property and profile, install the code in your blog, test to make sure that the installation was successful and find out how to get your first analytics report back.

In Part Four, you will be able to analyse your data. You'll find out what you need to take to a potential partner and how to find it in your analytics software. You will be able to find out who is coming to your blog, how often they return, which posts people are viewing most often and determine the split between new visitors and returning visitors. You will be able to start measuring with 100% accuracy the success of the strategies and campaigns you create to bring people to your blog.

I'll show you how to use analytics to leverage your data and attract sponsors you want to invest in your blog. By presenting your analytics professionally, you will be able to show advertisers why spending their advertising budgets on your blog will help them find their exact audience, answering any questions and addressing any concerns they may have about investing. It doesn't matter what your negotiating skills are like – advertisers recognise a good opportunity when they see it. You will be able create and share reports in your analytics that will show that you have the audience that advertisers want – how much you charge for it is your choice.

Part Five focuses on ad serving, why you need it and how to do it right. I'll walk you through the setup, execution and reporting processes involved in ad serving. Once you can do this, you will be able to deliver any type of advertising you could sell to a potential advertiser.

In Part Six, we will go through ad networks and exchanges and how you can leverage the power of these networks and exchanges on your own blog. We're going to delve into Google AdSense, showing you the exact setup, execution and reporting that you can achieve through this platform.

After completing Parts Five and Six, you will have a very powerful ad serving operation to monetise your blog instantly. You will be able to execute hybrid strategies, combining advertiser revenue with your Google AdSense revenue and I'll show you how you can create bespoke advertising areas within your blog where different advertisers can advertise in relevant sections of the site – an absolute must if you want to attract section-specific sponsors.

There's a lot to get through, so let's dive straight in.

Part 1:

Why you should be using analytics

Chapter 1:

What is web analytics going to do for me anyway and do I really need all this hassle?

When you're blogging and holding down a full-time life you have hundreds of things you already need to do, so what value will web analytics bring to you? By virtue of you having picked up this book, you know there is some value in web analytics and more than a dozen or so different analytics tools. But what precisely is the value and which tool should you use?

Let's start with the first question. Yes, there is a cost in terms of time and effort to implement analytics into your blog – it's a one-off cost (don't worry, I'll walk you through the process) and once implemented, you will have to spend time analysing your data. This book will help shorten both these time periods and any time you spend on analysis will be spent gaining valuable insight into what your audience want and need – and how your blog is (or isn't) meeting that need.

As much as it is a 'plug and play' process (or so the analytics companies selling their software will have you believe), the top level of analysis that comes back to you will be fairly generic. You'll need to dig deeper to really get the most out of your analytics software. Again, I'll show you the exact, step-by-step method to do this and the contextual relationships you would want to make between your metrics.

Once you have this data, you will really understand how your audience are interacting with your blog and that means going beyond how many pageviews you had last month and where those pageviews came from. The methods that I will present to you will help you understand the whole analytics platform and we will examine how you can create context for your analysis that demonstrates the value your blog holds. If those contextual metrics are weak, we can use other indicators to find out why and how to build up engagement in those areas.

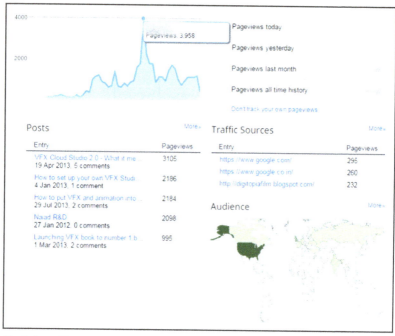

Fig 1.1 In Blogger, you can get a basic set of stats – don't confuse this with analytics.

You will be able to put your marketer hat on and know what value your blog has for a potential sponsor or advertiser. This goes way beyond setting up an AdSense account, which you may think is the easy option (I'll show you in Part Six of this book the quick and easy method to do this) but involves actually going directly to your preferred sponsor and pitching your blog as a platform to them. Believe me, this is not nearly as crazy as it sounds or as difficult to do once you have a set of analytics reports. The aim is to show potential sponsors that you have an audience that precisely matches their target market – they are already spending a hundred times more (in advertising spend) failing to capture this market than they can spend successfully with you, so using your analytics to show you have the audience that they want gives you the key to securing their advertising budget for your blog.

> **Fact #1:** *Advertisers have budgets to spend.*

Listen to any thought leader and they will tell you the same thing – advertisers are not getting the return on investment from traditional advertising channels that they need to survive. This is where the blogger comes in. But which bloggers should advertisers spend their budget on? The answer lies in who can prove that they have the audience. And that's where this book comes in – to show you how to harvest your analytics.

Even if you don't have the audience size that advertisers want, you still have an audience of some kind. You should still be able to make more of an income from even a small audience, especially if that audience is engaged with your content. If you think your audience size doesn't warrant approaching an advertiser, you can still use the data that you have to generate an income, using a mix of small advertising budgets and ad networks like AdSense. In fact, in Part Six of this book we'll see how you can set up your advertisers to use AdSense when you've served all the impressions that you've sold – or more accurately that advertisers have bought from you.

'But it's not all about the money,' I hear you say. 'It's about being free to say what you want to on your blog!'

You're completely correct; I couldn't agree with you more. Your blog is your space and your audience have come to you and keep coming back. None of us want to sell out to advertisers, but think of it this way: if you could make a reasonable income from your blog that involved only advertisers that you hand-picked, wouldn't that help you make your blog better? Wouldn't that allow you to dedicate more time to your blog and help your audience even more? Wouldn't you be able to spend more time finding new visitors that you could also help?

What this book is giving you is a means to approach companies in the form of a partnership. After all, you are interested in a company because your interests are aligned with theirs. Similarly, that company is equally interested in working with you, as you both share the same interests. Gone are the days where a multinational company would close their doors to you; today it's a two-way street and savvy companies know the value that a collection of bloggers can have.

Going back as far as 1957, Roy Thomson, former owner of *The Times*, described selling advertising as 'a licence to print money' (his actual quote was 'a permit to print money' – but it's often misquoted as a licence to print money).

I'm not suggesting you should blog solely for the sake of making money – that would be foolish – but the fact is that when you do something for the love of it and to help others, then success closely follows.

Why exactly should you miss out on that?

Advertisers are going to spend money anyway, so it may as well be with you!

ESSENTIAL WEB ANALYTICS FOR BLOGGERS

How to get more of the traffic you want and make money through banner advertising

Farhan Qureshi

About the Author

First and foremost, Farhan is a blogger from London, in the UK. For his day job, Farhan looks after all kinds of big client analytics. In his time, Farhan has looked after web analytics and ad serving operations for dozens of different brands, working directly with nearly 100 different advertisers on a daily basis. Farhan has been hands-on and brokered deals with advertisers to serve banner advertising on a wide variety of blogs. Using advanced web analytics platforms, he has been able to demonstrate the value each blog's audience has for advertisers, leading to very large-scale advertising deals brokered.

Farhan is passionate about helping bloggers gain the most traction out of their blogs. A blogger himself, he runs three successful blogs: www.digitopiaDigital.com, www.digitopiaFilm.com and www.workingParent.info in his spare time. Farhan believes and acts on the values that bloggers bring to a community – 'Bloggers are the last bastion of true independence; they are not driven by paymasters, or the need to hit quarterly targets. Bloggers are driven to share their knowledge and help their audience.'

For the first time, Farhan shares all the tactics and knowledge he has gained from running successful blogs, both large and small, from established, heavyweight, industry-respected blogs to zero-budget, high-energy start-up blogs.

Farhan is also a dad of two, holds down a full-time job as well as juggling blogging and filmmaking lives. He keeps himself busy...

About the Editor/Layout Designer

Vicki Watson is a writer, editor and book designer whose publications have ranged from business books, teacher resource guides and parental handbooks to children's fiction, stage plays and poetry. After a career as a teacher and deputy headteacher, she decided to focus on her love of language and design and set up Callisto Green, a vibrant and dynamic writing and design venture and small publishing imprint where she now spends her days playing with words and pictures.

When she's not scribbling in her notebook, her many interests include playing the clarinet, rock-climbing, stargazing and playing chess. She lives in Wiltshire with her husband and three sons.

Vicki can be contacted by emailing vicki@callistogreen.com or through her website at www.callistogreen.com.

About the Cover Designer

Cover designer Alex Mathers is also an illustrator, speaker, consultant and writer from London, born in Copenhagen in 1984. Having completed a geography degree in 2006, he is strongly influenced by the world around him and specialises in creating digital vector maps and landscapes.

Working with creative businesses, Alex improves marketing strategies so that his clients bring in more customers and achieve greater success.

Alex also runs an illustration platform called Ape on the Moon and a site called Red Lemon Club, for helping illustrators and other creatives to market themselves. It is through this site that he's self-published four books.

Alex can be contacted through his website at www.alexmathers.net/.

This book is dedicated to the memory of my sister. I took the tiniest fraction of the strength and bravery you showed, to get me to finish this book. You are my hero.

Contents

Chapter 2:

There are so many pieces of software to use. Which should I choose?

One of the first places that bloggers fall is when deciding which particular software to use. There's a large pool to choose from and each promises to be better than or different to the others.

Many of us fall into this analysis paralysis trap where we can spend all our time trying to figure out which one to use. Not only does this take so long to figure out, thus taking away precious blogging time, it also causes immense confusion and fatigue.

Fact #2: *The longer you take to choose your platform, the more valuable data you will be losing.*

There are so many players in the web analytics space that trying to go through and review them all is a fairly futile exercise, not least because the players are constantly changing and products constantly evolving. What I think is more important for you at this stage is to simply get started on one. There's absolutely no reason that you can't change platforms later, once you are more familiar with the analytics side of things. Similarly, you can also have more than one analytics software running on your blog, giving you the ability to compare directly and see which works best for you.

The features offered by most current products are reasonably similar. At the outset, the offerings were significantly different but now that most providers realise what users want to analyse, the differences between the products is more to do with the speed at which you can view, analyse and report on your data.

In fairness to each of the products, the speed at which you may initially do this will vary, so it is the steepness of the learning curve that should interest you more. For example, Product B may claim to be faster than Product A, but once you have invested time to learn the workflow in Product A, it won't take you too long at all. Whichever product you use, the important thing is usability. You will develop speed and efficiency as you go on.

Although each platform will have a list of USPs (Unique Selling Points), right now you want to install something that is:

- Quick
- Free
- Easy

For my own two blogs, I use Google Analytics precisely because it is quick, free and easy. More than likely it may be what you have installed or are considering installing. For the purposes of being able to establish and present what value my blog has for advertisers, this does an excellent job and is universally recognised. This wide recognition is important and will actually build confidence in potential advertisers when they look at your figures. For the purposes of this book, I'll use Google Analytics as the demonstration platform, but the same principles hold true for whichever analytics platform you choose to use.

Chapter 3:

But it's too difficult; I don't have the time.

I know where you are coming from on this. In order to get a blog up and running there are countless tasks to be done, and even if it is relatively well-established, there are still plenty of other jobs to do to keep a blog up and running. So when exactly are you going to find time to install the software, let alone actually use it?

Without knowing how to do this, it could take a fair amount of time to figure out. In Chapter 11, I'll show you how to generate the code and where to install it. It is genuinely a one-off, five-minute job (essentially it's copy and paste), though knowing where to copy and paste takes longer.

Once you have the analytics set up, it's going to take some time to sift through all the information that is coming your way. There's going to be a lot of data to analyse, all of which can give you valuable insight. But given that you are a blogger and not an analyst, you don't want to be spending all your time analysing the data. After all, you have a blog to maintain. And since we all have different types of blog and are trying to achieve something different and unique, the analytics that we need from them will be different and unique too. In Chapter 21, I'll show you how to create dashboards that will auto-populate with the data that is most valuable to your type of blog.

It's unrealistic to expect that the plug-and-play option will be adequate for your purposes. You are going to have to dedicate a bit of time to create a set-up that reflects the goals of your blog and it may even take a few iterations to get it right. But once you have, you can automate that process so that you receive monthly reports back. If you want to dive in further, you'll have the fluency to do that too. That is the whole premise of this book – there are a lot of things to do to get the analytics on the blog up and running; there are a lot of things that can be automated; some of these are five-minute jobs and others are more involved. What I am giving you in this book is a structured, step-by-step method to do all these tasks and make it work for you.

I am going to take you through all these tasks in a way that you will be able to understand and customise to suit your own particular purposes. Whilst I walk you through each step, you will gain a wider confidence to ask and answer any question about your blog. This book gives you the ability to figure out what is working and what isn't working on your own blog and how you can fix it.

Part 2:

How to use your
analytics to
make money from your blog

Chapter 4:

The three-step WAB formula: Implement, Analyse and Present.

I've developed a simple process for you to quickly and easily go from start to finish in your endeavour to fully integrate analytics into your blog:

Step 1 – Implement the analytics code

Step 2 – Analyse the data

Step 3 – Refine and present the data

It's really simple and this process forms the backbone of the book. We've spoken about how easy Step 1 will be and how it is a one-off cost. Chapter 11 will show you step-by-step how to do this.

Analysing your data is both about finding out where your blog is excelling and establishing the areas it needs to improve upon. Let's take an example. You may find that you are getting a lot of visitors each month from a search engine (Google, Bing etc.). 'Great,' you think. 'I'm an SEO (Search Engine Optimisation) maestro!' True, your SEO may be great, so you show this to advertisers, only to have them point out that your Bounce Rate (i.e. those visitors who view only one page before leaving) is also very high. It's therefore vital to know and understand all the terms in your analytics report so that you can see where you need to focus your attention.

Analysing also means thinking in terms of what opportunity your blog holds for potential advertisers. What is it they are looking for and how can you fulfil that need? For instance, you may blog about the best fishing spots in Brighton and from your analytics find that 80% of your visitors are living in the Brighton area. That demographic of keen fishers who live in Brighton would be very valuable for the fishing equipment shops in the town, so you might choose to write a post about best fishing supply shops in the area and sell links directly to those shops either through:

- a tenancy ad (a fixed cost the advertiser pays to have their ad on the page, regardless of whether anyone clicks on it or not);
- a CPM (Cost per Mile) ad, where the advertiser pays to have their advert shown a pre-determined number of times, e.g. 10,000 impressions;
- a PPC (Pay per Click) ad where the advertiser pays only when people click on their ad;
- an affiliate scheme where you take a fixed percentage of any resulting sale made by a visitor (this is also sometimes known as a CPA (Cost per Acquisition)) or
- a CPV (Cost per View) ad where the advertiser pays you for anyone who views their video – whether the viewer takes action or not, you get paid if the video is viewed.

However you choose to leverage your blog, the point is that you wouldn't even know you had this opportunity without first having access to the data.

Let's take another example, this time of lead generation.

Say you run a tourist blog about the best things to do when visiting Hastings and your blog contains a 'plan your visit' section where you provide suggested itineraries of how to make the most of your visit. In this scenario, the majority of your site visitors don't actually live in Hastings, *but by visiting the 'plan your visit' section they've expressed an interest in planning a visit to Hastings* – why else would they have visited and explored your site in so much depth?

If based on what you have written they do actually visit Hastings, then you yourself will not directly gain anything other than helping people make the most of their trip. But you can help yourself and help visitors further by either displaying adverts for local restaurants or advising them directly on which restaurants are close to particular historical areas of interest, maybe even giving each a rating.

Having access to how many people are viewing these pages and which pages they viewed before/after along their journey in your site, you can demonstrate to local businesses that you have an audience who are planning a trip to the local area. Here your blog has the chance to help local businesses too (who may otherwise be swept away by the global franchises that operate in the area).

There are so many areas where your analytics can take you. You may decide to have an online booking service to the local restaurants or a newsletter sign up with a 10% off food voucher (since we all know restaurants make higher margins on drinks). The visitor prints off the voucher and takes it to the restaurant on their day out. Now you and the advertised restaurant can directly measure the success of your blog's influence. You can show how many times that voucher was downloaded and the restaurant can measure how many people came in with that voucher. The restaurant is savvy enough to know that you are bringing in 50 vouchers a week where the average spend (after discounts) is £30. That equates to £1,500 that your blog is directly bringing to that restaurateur per week. How much are you going to charge to have that printable voucher on your blog?

In my own case, one of the blogs that I run, www.digitopiafilm.com, hosts a series of short 3D software tutorials – one of them I've titled 'The Maya to Houdini Conversion Course', where I teach VFX and CG artists how they can do the same things in Houdini that they can do in Maya (two high-end, 3D software tools). My goal here is to help artists make the transition across, but at the same time I can see there is an opportunity to approach the big, online tutorial providers to directly advertise in this space. Sure, I could use AdSense and target the keywords 'animation', '3D' etc., but that's no guarantee that I will get 3D tutorial services advertising in these slots. I may if I'm lucky get some other 3D software provider appear here (although I'll show you in Chapter 29 how to target contextual advertising through

AdSense). But every ad slot that goes unfilled by a 3D animation/VFX school is a huge missed opportunity. After all, visitors have clearly expressed what is called an 'intent to buy' – in this case they chose through whatever channel (it may have been through a search engine, a tweet, LinkedIn link or through navigating my blog) to watch a video to help them learn Houdini. So wouldn't it make sense for me to place an advert for an online school where the visitor could learn more? That way I'd be providing immense value to both my visitor and the school.

This is another example of targeting. In this case it has nothing to do with geographical location but more in terms of their interest, specifically their interest in learning the 3D animation software Houdini. Notice the significant difference, they are interested in 'learning 3D software' rather than having a general interest in '3D software'. It may seem subtle on the surface, but knowing that they want to *learn* will help me leverage better returns for my advertiser (in this case animation schools rather than animation software providers based on the word 'learning').

The point is that the type of analytics that you need will be unique to the goals of your blog – what you are trying to achieve will largely determine the type of data you need to filter. So before you even begin to think about deploying analytics to your blog, establish what it is you are trying to achieve. Let's step through this together.

- Are you a content site? Do people come to you for your expertise on a particular subject?
- Are you trying to sell something through your site? If so, are you selling:
    * Products?
    * Services?
    * Expertise?

Let's look at various scenarios.

If you have a content blog, people are coming to your site to consume the stories and posts you are putting up. Your aim here is have a constant and hopefully huge flow of traffic through your site.

Why would this be your aim?

Well apart from the obvious that you want to help people with your great content, the secondary benefit here is that the more traffic you have, the better you will be able to attract the right kind of sponsor to your website.

> **Fact #3:** *Advertisers follow eyeballs. The more interested and engaged those eyeballs are with your content, the better it is for you and your advertiser.*

Your analytics will demonstrate that you have both a substantial and engaged audience. There are so many ways that you can do this. Let's say that you run a health and fitness blog. In this case, your analytics may tell you that you have a large audience in the New York area that are interested in learning about Kung Fu. For that particular section of your site, you could sell advertising directly to Kung Fu schools in the New York area (I'll show you in Chapter 25 how to target the advertising based on the visitor's location). On another part of your blog, you might see that you have a large UK following on vitamins in pregnancy. Here, you may choose to sell your advertising to one of the large pharmacy chains in the UK.

The sections of your blog will tell you instantly what your audience are interested in – it's more than reasonable to say that anyone who visits four individual blogs posts on 'Kung Fu for Beginners' is someone interested in Kung Fu with little or no experience. You can make your posts even more granular by posting a series of articles on 'Self-Defence for Women'. Again, you know that visitors in this part of the blog are women who want to learn about self-defence. Using your analytics to find out the geographical location of those visitors will help you sell advertising in different cities to target this niche (we'll go step-by-step exactly how you do the whole process). If at the end of each post you have a newsletter sign up where visitors can learn more, you can then measure (by way of the number of sign-ups) active engagement, i.e. where a visitor did more than read the post but took some action based on your advice. This gives you 'authority', something that advertisers are looking for.

Advertisers spend money promoting their businesses on the sides of buses and on billboards, and often this gains them little to no traction. You can demonstrate that you already have the audience an advertiser wants and that in a single step (in the shape of a click), the audience can go directly to the company.

Let's look in the next chapter how analytics will actually help you monetise your blog.

Chapter 5:

How will analytics actually help you make money out of your traffic?

Before we answer this question, let's clear up two definitions which will help you clarify your strategy going forward. The word 'traffic' can have two broad meanings:

- visitors – how many people came to your website in a given time period and

- pageviews – how many pages those visitors viewed over any given amount of time.

There is a significant difference between the two concepts. The first would tell an advertiser that your blog has 1,000 people visit the site over a month, for example, whereas the second tells that advertiser that 1,000 pages were viewed last month.

Neither metric (a metric is something that can be measured) tells you anything about the other. For instance, were the 1,000 pageviews viewed by one visitor, by two visitors or by 1,000 individual visitors? In the same way, did the 1,000 visitors visit 1,000 pages, 10,000 or 100,000 pages between them?

> **Fact #4:** *One metric on its own doesn't tell the whole story.*

There is also a significant difference between a visitor and a unique visitor, a pageview and a unique pageview, and we're going to get into all the definitions and what they mean in the subsequent chapters. I don't want to bog you down in those details (just yet), but I do want to introduce you to the different considerations that will define your strategy.

The second definition I want to present at this point is that of Click Through Rate, otherwise known as CTR. You're going to hear the term CTR thrown about with reckless abandon throughout your blogging adventure, which is why it's important to understand exactly what it means at the start. In this way, you can define strategies to attain high CTRs at the outset and save yourself a lot of time. High CTRs also lead to happy advertisers and happy affiliate partners who will want to keep coming back to you to buy more advertising.

Let's break this into its constituent parts:

- A 'click through' occurs when someone clicks on an advertising banner on your site which subsequently leads the user to the advertiser's website.

- That visitor is now visiting your advertiser's site.

- That visitor would not have visited the advertiser's site had you not have taken him/her there.

- The advertiser wouldn't have accomplished this on their own.

- It's down to you that a particular visitor has landed on the advertiser's site and

- You deserve the credit for it, therefore you deserved to be compensated for taking the visitor to the advertiser's site.

A 'rate', as the name suggests, is the percentage of how many impressions of an advert were clicked through to the advertiser's site. The CTR is calculated as a percentage as follows:

$$CTR = (banner\ ad\ clicks / impressions)\ x\ 100$$

For example, let's say that 1 banner ad click occurred after 100 ad impressions were delivered. In this case, the CTR would be as follows:

$$(1\ click\ /\ 100\ impressions)\ x\ 100 = 1\%\ CTR$$

Let's define what an 'impression' is before we go on. Firstly:

- An impression is neither a user nor a pageview.
- An impression is when an advert is shown on a page.

Really? Does that deserve a definition of its own?

Well actually, yes it does. You may have a few different locations on your page to serve ads (some recommend that you have no more than three ads on a page and I tend to agree with that; sites with more than three tend to look a bit spammy) – typically you may have a Leader Board (728px x 90px) at the top of the page and two rectangular ad units on the right side further down the page.

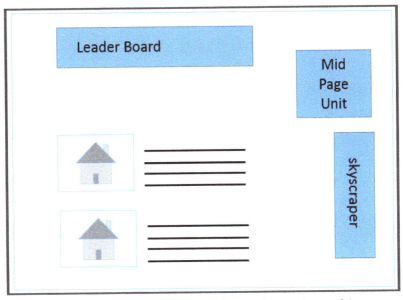

Fig 5.1 Typical ad units on your page. The Leader Board sits at the top of the page (although sometimes you may put it/another one below the article, just above the share buttons), the Mid-Page Unit (often referred to as a MPU) can go on the side or within the body of the article and the Skyscrapers (known imaginatively as a Sky) tends to go down the side of the page.

If a visitor lands on a page that only has a single leader board from your advertiser, then your ad serving software will record that as one impression.

You may well have placed three ad units on your page, but if the advertiser only provides a single creative (in this example a leader board), then that would be only one ad impression. If the advertiser provides three creatives (a leader board, a MPU and a Skyscraper) and those three are seen together on one pageview, then that would count as three ad impressions, i.e. in that case, one pageview equals three ad impressions.

There are different methods to predict what your CTR may be:

- You could take an industry average.
- You could take an average for your particular sector/type of blog.
- You could use your own historical data which you'll build up over a few months.

Establishing your CTR will help you understand what you can reasonably expect at the start of your approach to advertisers. To keep the calculations simple, let's say you have a CTR of 10% (if you do have a CTR of 10% you are doing incredibly well!) and you get an average of 1,000 pageviews a month, serving on average two impressions per pageview, i.e. you serve 2000 impressions a month.

The CTR will tell you that:

2000 impressions x 10% CTR = 200 click throughs to your advertiser(s)

The question you need to ask is what is 200 clicks to my advertiser worth?

There are lots of ways you can establish this. One method is to calculate:

a) The average purchase price of the product/service my advertiser is selling.

b) The probability that the visitor will purchase through the advertiser's site, i.e. the advertiser's conversion rate.

Let's look at two examples of how this could work.

You run a financial advice website and your advertiser is a stocks and shares company. The landing page the advertiser gives you has a minimum purchase of £1,000 on a new share fund they've launched; their page has a time-limited offer of no fees if the visitor signs up now.

Let's say that half the people who visit end up buying the minimum £1,000 portfolio. That means that each person you bring to the company's site has a 0.5 probability to purchase a £1,000 portfolio.

You therefore deduce that the click is worth £500 (i.e. £1,000 x 0.5).

Now that you've calculated that each click is worth £500, the question is how you negotiate that share of the money with your advertiser. This is where your analytics becomes so valuable.

Another example would be if your advertiser owns a nappy website where the average purchase value is £5 and the conversion probability is 0.1 (i.e. 10% of people who visit end up buying the nappy on offer). Unlike the 'no fee', time-limited offer, you can buy nappies anywhere, so you deduce the value to be fifty pence (i.e. £5 x 0.1 probability = £0.5).

Here your analytics will need to be used differently to negotiate your share of the money – you need to prove to the advertiser that you have the exact audience they are trying to reach and negotiate a higher rate for their advertising. That rate could come in various forms, and you could use the following techniques to negotiate a price:

- A CPM (Cost per Mile) model, where you charge a fixed amount of money to deliver the ads. Note that we said 'deliver' – we are only guaranteeing ad delivery, not subsequent sales.
    * Main pro: you will get paid regardless of whether anyone clicks on the ads or not.
    * Main con: you may have to accept a lower rate, but at least you are guaranteed payment.

- A CPC (Cost Per Click) model, where you only get paid per click of the creative, essentially letting the advertiser have free advertising.

  * Main pro: you can negotiate a higher rate per click.

  * Main con: you may receive nothing, since if no one clicks, you don't get paid

  * If you go for this model, be sure to have high confidence levels that visitors will click the adverts

- A CPA (Cost per Acquisition) model, where you only get paid if someone actually buys the product or goods on offer.

  * Main pro: you can negotiate a really high rate for each acquisition made. In the example of the financial investment portfolio, your share of a single acquisition of a portfolio could be more than you would earn in a whole month using a CPM model.

  * Main con: you could end up with nothing – you are essentially dependent upon how well the advertiser converts any traffic you send them (assuming anyone actually clicks on the ads in the first place). The worst-case scenario is that you end up giving away free advertising.

  * If you go for this model, be confident that your visitors will both click on the adverts and that the advertiser's landing page (where they accept the offer) is strong enough to convert the visitor into a buyer and that monetary value is satisfactory for you.

Whichever model you choose, your analytics will put you in a better negotiating position. These analytics will show the advertiser that you have exactly the audience they are after. When they understand this, then you are in the stronger position. They have the product, but you have the audience, and if they want that audience then there should be a fair price paid for it. Of course the advertiser knows that you could offer that same advertising space to their competitors too.

One technique I have used is to place AdSense ads onto the page and send a screen grab to a company to show how their advertising would look in situ. Of course I browsed their main competitor's site for a while and waited for the AdSense algorithms to kick in before making the screen grabs. When my first choice advertiser saw that the advertising could go to his competitor, the deal swung dramatically in my favour. It's like a double-ended light sabre – on the one side you have the promise of the advertiser's exact audience, and on the other side the advertiser knows you could take that audience to their competitor. Either way, what you are looking for is a fair price for your advertising.

In the next chapter we'll explore further how you can dive into your analytics to determine what you can offer to your advertiser.

Part 6:

Chapter 27:

Chapter 28:

Chapter 29:

Chapter 30:

Chapter 31:

Part 7:

Chapter 32:

Chapter 33:

Chapter 6:

Using analytics to determine what you can offer to potential partners.

There are many different ways to make money from your blog, from selling your own products, working with affiliate marketing or aiming to generate advertising revenue. However you intend to make money from your blog, your analytics will help you:

- Set milestone targets to help you understand how near (or far) you are to reaching your overall goal.

- Understand what strategy is best suited to your website as it currently stands.

- Assess the effectiveness of your marketing efforts.

- Identify what you need to change in your marketing mix to reach each milestone.

Let's return to our example of the high-end financial products blog. We deduced that a click through to our advertiser's website was worth £500, i.e. the minimum buying price is £1,000 of a particular portfolio and they (your advertiser) convert 50% of people who visit their site. How would you use your analytics to prove that the advertiser should buy advertising on your site and at what price should you be charging them?

Let's start from a worst-case scenario and say that you have very little traffic flowing through your website. Does that mean that you should follow the knee-jerk reaction that many so-called experts give and not approach an advertiser? On the contrary, looking into your analytics will tell you how close you are to approaching advertisers. If you have low traffic, the first metric to look at is the engagement level of your current audience.

'Engagement' essentially means:

- Are your visitors engaging with your content?
- Are they reading lots of your posts?
- How many posts do they read on average?
- How much time do they spend reading your posts?
- Do they leave comments at the end of your posts?
- Are they sharing your content on social media (Tweets, Likes, +1s are strong 'social signals')?
- Which part of the posts are they reading?
- If you have video, are they watching the video?
- Are they signing up to your latest financial asset newsletter?

Your analytics report will show you exactly how your audience is engaging with your content. If you find that your visitors are reading about four posts per visit, watching your videos, commenting and starting discussions with you and other visitors below your posts, you have two highly sought-after qualities on your site – that of 'authority' and 'engagement'. People clearly respect your content enough to leave comments, perhaps even ask you questions about finance products and are starting discussions that are influencing others to buy or not buy a particular product. For advertisers, this is of crucial importance.

Fact #5: *Once you have influence online, you will be in a much stronger negotiating position with advertisers.*

It may just be the case that your particular subject matter has a limited audience or that you haven't spent enough time on SEO (Search Engine Optimisation) or marketing. But you can show your advertiser that visitors are clearly interested and that you can send qualified traffic to their website.

Imagine that you run an authoritative ship-building website and you send one highly qualified visitor to your ball bearing's manufacturer who ends up spending a million dollars on an order. The quality of your visitors is there in your reports. Firstly the visitor chose to come to your financial products/ship-building website and secondly they chose to read three articles, demonstrating an interest in the product. If you target a particular ad (and I'll show you how to target an ad against a piece of content in Chapter 25), the fact that the visitor choses to click on the ad shows a clear intent to buy.

Fact #6: *Smaller groups of highly qualified traffic are more valuable than large groups of unqualified traffic.*

You can demonstrate engagement by creating a dashboard comprised of various metrics including:

- pages per visit
- duration on website
- average time spent on each page
- social shares
- comments

I'll show you how to create these dashboards in Chapter 21, but for now I want to get you thinking of which metrics are important to you, rather than worrying and giving up because you don't have a huge amount of traffic. It's better to have a small amount of engaged traffic than a huge disinterested audience. Think quality of visitor over quantity of visitors.

The number of visitors and pageviews your blog is attracting is meaningless when viewed in isolation. The whole point of analytics and this book is to look at metrics in their context and establish value in your web traffic. It's this audience value that is going to push your blog ahead and generate more revenue for you, regardless of which methods you use. (In this particular book I am pushing ahead with advertising revenue, but the same use of your analytics will help you negotiate better rates if affiliate marketing is your thing and it will certainly help sell more of your own products, which I do on my blogs too.)

When you can put a value on your web traffic, you can leverage that value with your advertiser, proving that you have the exact audience they are seeking and selling the ability to reach their target audience. The fact that you will charge less than an advertising agency would is an added boon.

Let's look at the flip side of the coin, and assume that you have a huge audience – tens of thousands of visitors on your site. Your first thought might be, 'Bam! I can serve ads straight away. In fact, I'll throw some AdSense ads on my site and wait for the money to gush in!' You wait, you wait and you wait some more and still nothing.

Why? After all, you have the traffic and you have relevant ads on your site (more on this in Chapter 27), but still nothing.

So you now decide to look at your analytics and find out what people are doing on your website. To start with, you'd like to know:

- Who are the visitors coming to the site?
- Are they new visitors or are they returning visitors?
- How many of them bounce, i.e. look at one page and leave?
- How are they getting to your site in the first place?
- Where (i.e. geographical location) are they coming from?

Many experts will tell you that a high bounce rate is the same as someone coming into your shop, taking one look and going, 'Uggghhh,' before leaving and never returning. Yet this is not always true. In fact, if you hear an expert telling you this, i.e. that a bounce is a bad thing, put her on the spot and ask, 'Why?'

Let's step through an example where a bounce is not always a bad thing.

➜ You put out a tweet about #financialFreedom.

- → Someone clicks on it and lands on your page.
- → On the landing page is an article with a link to an affiliate partner's product.
- → The visitor reads the article and decides to click on the partner's link.
- → The link then takes them to the partner's site, where they sign up and you earn your commission.

Now this whole process will count as a bounce in your analytics. Yet someone came onto your blog, viewed one page and left, but in this case, a bounce to your partner's site was exactly what you wanted.

For example, say a particular landing page with an external link has a bounce rate of 80% and you set up an 'event' on that link which shows that 80% of traffic on that page clicks the link you provide, e.g. signs up for an affiliate offer. All of a sudden that 80% bounce rate and one page per visit doesn't look too bad – it means 80% of visitors who landed there did exactly what you asked them to do.

In Chapter 20, I will show you how to set up events so you can differentiate between a bounce and an interaction which leads someone away from your website, like signing up for a newsletter or clicking on an affiliate link.

First find out which of your landing pages have the highest bounce rate (a 'landing page' is where people land on your site). This page may be a page that links to an external piece of content, i.e. a video or a link to an affiliate. Then set up any external links as events (see Chapter 20 for how to do this). In the 'event' you create, you have an option to define a 'non interaction', i.e. do not count leaving my blog on this page as a bounce.

Doing this correctly across your blog will give you a truer measure of your bounce rate. No analytics platform does this out of the box; it wouldn't be possible. So the onus is on you to define links and give them event names. You can obviously extrapolate this further yourself and change what would otherwise have been counted as a bounce into a meaningful goal value (to which you can attribute a monetary value).

> **Fact #7:** *One single metric does not tell the whole story; you need to put metrics into the correct context.*

One single metric does not and cannot tell the whole story and the problem with many analytics software is that the headline information (the top-level metrics that you see) can be misunderstood all too easily. It's not the fault of the analytics software. After all they have to present something to you when you login, and who wouldn't want to give their user an immediate snapshot of their site? But the problem is that bloggers are not delving deep enough into the analytics to understand and tell the whole story of their blog.

The following chapters are going to go really in-depth to show you which metrics will help you understand your users' journeys, and how you can extract and present this data to get the whole picture of what is happening on your site and how you can improve upon it.

Chapter 7:

Deciding which story to tell, finding your weak points and developing strategies to improve them.

There are always two sides to every story – you've heard the phrase before. But hidden away in your analytics are many hundreds of stories that you could tell. When selling advertising directly you will need to consider:

- which story you want to tell
- which story your sponsors/partners want to hear

Not all of the hundreds of metrics available will be telling a rosy story of your blog. In fact, the most valuable of your metrics will be the ones that tell a negative tale. Yes, it is disheartening to know that only 10% of your visitors are returning visitors, but knowing the issues with your website will help you to focus your energy and efforts on fixing them. After we've learnt how to set up and gather the data (Chapters 10 and 11), we'll look at strategies to improve various metrics, as there are different solutions to different underperforming metrics.

At this stage (before diving into installing and analysing analytics), it's very important to ascertain your goals for your blog. If you want to make money from your blog, you will need to ask yourself the following questions:

- How much money do I want to earn from my blog?
- How many visitors or pageviews do I need to generate on my blog to earn that amount of money?

- How do those visitors need to interact with my site? Do I need them to:
  - Click on a banner ad?
  - Leave their e-mail address?
  - Fill out a form?
  - Refer a friend?
  - Download a product?
- Where can I find the audience that I need and what methods work best to bring them to my blog?
- What is it that this audience needs and what problem are they struggling with that I can solve?

You need to identify specific behaviour or a range of behaviours that the visitor needs to complete for you to meet your goal(s). Once you define this, then you can find the answer within your analytics and show it to your advertising partners.

For example, you may run a website about car repairs. If you show that you have 5000 pageviews on your page about replacing car exhausts and see that people are leaving questions and comments on how useful this post was, then you can go to a car exhaust supplier in any area (I'll show you how to serve local ads for advertisers to match the visitor's locality in Chapter 25) and match their ad to a very precise subject where people have shown interest.

This in itself is a major sign to the advertiser that your website:
- has visitors who are engaged in the content so much so that they are willing to load a second page to get answers to their questions;
- is providing solutions and
- could, together with the advertiser's products, be part of the solution.

If you break the post into two posts with a 'read more' link at the bottom of the first half leading to the second half, then you can show what percentage of people who viewed the first page actually go on to reading the second page. If lots of people are going on to that second page it shows a very high engagement level. Equally valuable to know is if people aren't going onto the second page.

There's actually a significant paradigm shift here in that these ratios tell you how well your content is engaging the audience. You could then of course write longer articles and break them into three or four parts, staggering the release of each part by a week. If you are really savvy you could at the end of Part 1, write something like, 'Make sure you check out Part 2 which I'll be releasing next week – to be the first to read it, subscribe to my list here'.

Now all of a sudden you are gathering even more valuable data and getting people to come back to your website to read the second, third and fourth parts. I'd say that's a pretty engaged readership, and the paradigm again shifts from, 'Would you like to buy advertising on my blog?' to 'How much will you spend advertising on my blog?' It's a great shift to occur.

You may run a parenting website like mine (www.workingParent.info), which includes a page to search for activities like playgroups in your area. The sort of thing where a visitor can enter their postcode (zip code) and a list of local playgroups appears.

With this sort of page, you can show:

a)   how many people visit that page

b)   how many people enter their postcode

c)   what those postcodes are

d)   how many click on the result to go the playgroup details page

There's a lot of valuable information here, from what the visitor's area of interest is (e.g. playgroup, swimming class, maths tuition), what their geographical location is and which results generate the most interest.

Both of these examples demonstrate a very important concept in analytics, that of 'the funnel'. The funnel is essentially the process a visitor takes to reach a certain goal, the number of visitors who drop out of the process and at which points they drop out. You will learn more about the funnel as you progress. For now, you need to know that there exists a funnel (process) that your visitors are taking to make a successful transaction and what proportion of your visitors are successfully completing that process to meet your and your advertiser's goals.

The point of this chapter is that telling yourself and your advertiser a story is more than set dressing negative analytics and that as your metrics evolve over time, there are a range of solutions to take your blog from one level to another. As you transition your blog upwards, there are different ways to monetise your blog at each stage of its evolution. We'll talk more about the solutions at each stage in Parts 4, 6 and 7. What you want to avoid is the 'my blog's not ready to monetise yet' syndrome, which prevents many from pushing their blog to its full potential.

Your blog is going to take time to develop to its final form or what you currently think its final form should be. Really, there is no final form that your blog will take (unless you jettison it). It will keep evolving and growing as you grow. The time it takes to go from one form to another is different for each blog and each blogger and your analytics will help you to determine the velocity at which your blog transforms.

The concept of velocity is actually an interesting one and you'll perhaps remember from your science classes that velocity is made up from two components - speed and direction. Neither of these in isolation will tell you much. You may be moving at great speed but unless you know in which direction you are heading, you won't know if you're going to hit your target (notwithstanding that your target will always be moving and evolving too). The same holds for the direction – you want to avoid moving very quickly in the wrong direction. Your analytics will help you determine both of these. The key thing to know is what you are trying to discover. Once you're clear on this, I'll show you how to use your analytics to answer your questions.

Chapter 8:

Delivering on your promises.

Using your analytics to directly approach advertisers comes from a position of honesty. You may not have the traffic you need yet, you may not have the engagement you need yet, but by using your analytics you will be able to see where you are in terms of traffic and engagement. You'll be able to see how far you need to progress and then measure the success of your strategy to get there. If you can show a progression towards the traffic or engagement levels you need, then your advertisers will know that they can come in on the ground floor and partner with you earlier in the process.

You may want to achieve at least 5,000 unique pageviews before approaching any advertising opportunity, be that from a direct advertiser or from using an ad exchange service like Google AdSense. If you can get closer to 10,000 pageviews a month then an advertiser will become really interested. Whatever your target is, your analytics will tell you if it's achievable or unambitious – and maybe you can even set the bar higher.

But why pageviews? Shouldn't I use visitors or sessions?

Well I deliberately phrased it this way because I wanted you to ask yourself these questions.

- What is the main difference between pageviews, visitors and sessions?
- Which of these should I use?

Let's look at the differences between these three top-level metrics.

- A pageview, as the name suggests, is the number of times a page on your blog loads.

- A visitor is a person from a unique IP address surfing your site.

- A session is the period of time that visitor engages (surfs) with your site.

For example, Sam logs onto your site at 10am on Monday morning, he browses two pages and leaves. Sam comes back at midday and browses three pages this time. What will your analytics show?

Monday will show as:

- 1 visitor (Sam)

- 2 sessions and

- 5 pageviews

If on Tuesday Joanne and Yurgi visit your site, Joanne surfs four pages and Yurgi sees one page before leaving, Tuesday will show as:

- 2 visitors (Joanne and Yurgi)

- 2 sessions and

- 5 pageviews

In both examples you achieved five pageviews but in very different ways. Is it better to have one visitor generate five pageviews or to have two visitors generate five pageviews?

You could argue for either. Monday's stats show that you have one highly engaged visitor but Tuesday shows that you had more visitors to your site, even though one of them bounced.

Either way, the common denominator is that you had five pageviews. This pageview figure directly translates to ad impressions. For example, if you have three banner ads on a single page* then 1 pageview = 3 ad impressions and maybe you have a wallpaper ad too. This is the currency you will trade for banner advertising. Whether it's to one or two visitors, the fact is that the pageview figure is directly linked to the ad impressions figure, whereas neither the visitors or sessions figures correspond directly to ad impressions.

For example, say you have 5 pageviews.

- Each page has 3 ads, so over 5 pages you display 15 ad impressions.

- Each page has a wallpaper impression (you sell the wallpaper/goalpost/skin as a premium, since it is one of the best converting ad units) – over 5 pages you display 5 wallpaper ad impressions.

- Over 5 pageviews you displayed a total of 20 ad impressions (i.e. 15 banner ads and 5 wallpaper ads).

It's these ad impressions that are most valuable to your advertising partners.

Whether these twenty ad impressions are shown to Sam on Monday or split between Joanne and Yurgi on Tuesday is of secondary importance; the executive summary you need to show your advertiser is that twenty ad impressions were served.

It's up to you to determine the value of one visitor viewing twenty ad impressions or two visitors viewing twenty ad impressions and at this early stage it's probably too much for your advertising partner to digest. After all, they have their own business to run.

---

* You could have more than three ads on one page but I'd recommend not to. More than three ads on a page saturates your page with advertising and takes away from the content, plus there are other valuable goals that you can put in your sidebars, like acquiring Twitter/Facebook/Google+ followers, having people join your mailing list and so on. Currently, three ad units is the maximum that most ad exchange programmes allow for.

Chapter 9:

How much value do you put on your first deal?

It's quite likely that when you are ready to approach an advertiser for that first deal, you will feel anxious over how much you should initially ask for. Obviously you have a target of what revenue you want but what if you can't deliver a reasonable return to your partner? You don't want to lose them on your first attempt. It would be hard to recover and have them build a long-term relationship with you if you deliver a poor return on the first month of advertising.

So should you go in with an introductory offer as it's their first time advertising with you and your first time advertising with anyone (whether you tell them that or not is another decision to make)?

The answer is to get some data behind you and base your figure on some real stats. I suggest once you hit your monthly target for pageviews (i.e. 5,000 or better yet 10,000 per month), start putting up advertising from an ad exchange platform like Google AdSense (others do exist and we'll discuss in Chapter 27) and start measuring the impressions served and the click through rates these adverts deliver. In Chapter 29, I will show you how to ensure that you have context-sensitive ads appear using the settings in Google AdSense. From here you will have a base figure of impressions, clicks and most importantly how much revenue you make from Google AdSense.

Bear in mind that:

a)   The revenue you get from AdSense is your share of what the advertiser actually pays to have the ad display on your site. The advertiser pays Google directly and Google gives you your share of the total, (currently (August 2015) you get 68% and Google gets 32%).

b) This is mostly done on a Pay Per Click model, i.e. the advertiser only pays when someone clicks, otherwise they are showing their advert free on your website. There are CPM models on AdSense but the amount of money you make from a single ad on a CPM model is paltry.

c) You should not be selling on a PPC model. Ideally you want to sell on a CPM model whereby you sell impressions, not clicks. Obviously don't turn down a good PPC offer, though; at this early stage, you may not be able to broker a CPM deal.

The third point allows you to get paid regardless of whether the advertiser gets any clicks or not. And yes, it can be done. I do it every day and so do countless others. Advertisers will recognise the opportunity your analytics and attribution models are presenting them.

Obviously you do have to get those clicks to maintain a long-term relationship, but if you have the right advertiser against the right content, you should be able to get more clicks via the direct advertiser than you would get through even the best ad exchange networks – or at least this should be your target.

That concludes this part of the book. In the following sections, we are going to get really technical on setting up analytics on your blog, analysing the figures and creating dashboards and reports based on this data.

What I wanted to achieve from Part Two is that you have gained a real understanding of why it's an absolute must for you to run an analytics solution on your blog, the real value and competitive advantage that it will bring to you and why you are about to spend a reasonable amount of time incorporating analytics into your site. Don't worry – I'm going to hold your hand during this process. It may seem a daunting journey you're about to go on, but I will lead you though it step by step, explaining both how to do each part and how each step contributes to the process that we've discussed in this section.

Okay, ready to go?

Let's do this…

Part 3:

The technical stuff:
How to install Analytics

Chapter 10:

Setting up an account.

As we spoke about earlier, the analytics product that I'm going to walk you through here is Google Analytics. That's not because I think it is the best analytics platform for you but because it's quick and easy to install and it's also free.

Free! Yay!!! We all like free, right?

Just one caution to bear in mind – the data is being collected by Google and they themselves are benefiting too. If this is a problem for you we can look at other platforms, but whichever platform you use you will be going through the same process as we are going to step through here.

Before you can install the code on your site, you'll need to set up an account. Actually, you probably already have one. If you use any Google product (Gmail, YouTube, G+, Blogger etc.) then you already have a Google Analytics account. All you need to do is to activate it.

Go to http://www.google.com/analytics/.

In the top right corner is the option to 'Create an Account' or to 'Sign In'.

Fig 10.1 Sign in or create an Analytics account.

Whichever of the two options you choose, you will be taken to this page:

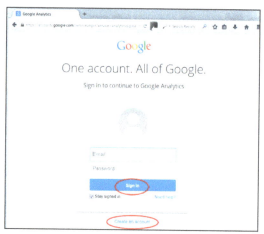

Fig 10.2 The sign-up page.

After creating an account in the usual way or by directly hitting 'Sign In', you'll be taken to a second screen asking you to sign up your account to start using Google Analytics – this is where you associate your Google account to the specific Analytics account.

Fig 10.3 Apparently there are only three steps to analyse your traffic – goes to show a sense of humour runs rife at Google!

Next you will come to a screen asking you to set the account and property details:

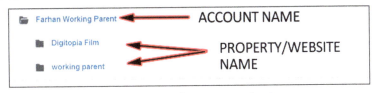

Fig 10.4 A few account details are entered here.You'll need to define whether it's a website or a mobile app.

There are two main things to set up here: the account name and the property details. It's a good idea to set the account as your business or your personal name, not the name of your blog. Although you may only have one blog at the moment, you may start more in the future. I fell into that hole myself when I set up Google Analytics the first time around.

Farhan Working Parent ◀━━━━━ **ACCOUNT NAME**

Digitopia Film

working parent

PROPERTY/WEBSITE NAME

Fig 10.5 You can associate numerous web properties under the same account name. Imagine that you start to run analytics for other people's sites — in that case you would set up different account names with their sites as the property name.

By mistake I called the Account 'Farhan Working Parent' for my site www.workingParent.info and then added 'working parent' as the property. Later on, when I installed Google Analytics into my film and animation blog www.digitopiafilm.com, I added this property to the same account name – it's not the end of the world as I know how to traverse the hierarchy, but there's no harm in doing it properly from the start (always good to learn from someone else's mistakes!).

Once you've entered all these details, you will see along the top bar the main sections of Google Analytics:

Fig 10.6 The top menu bar in Google Analytics.

- 'Home' will take you to the homepage (Fig 10.5),

- 'Reporting' will take you to all the cool analytics that you want (we won't go there just yet – see Chapters 14 to 21 for the juicy stuff),

- 'Customization' will help you build custom reports that are not readily available in Google Analytics out of the box, I'll show you in Chapters 15 to 21 which customisations could work best for your blog

- 'Admin' is where the boring but totally necessary details live to get your analytics from your blog - this whole section is focused on how to get this set up correctly

Clicking 'Admin' will take you to the administration page, which will look like this:

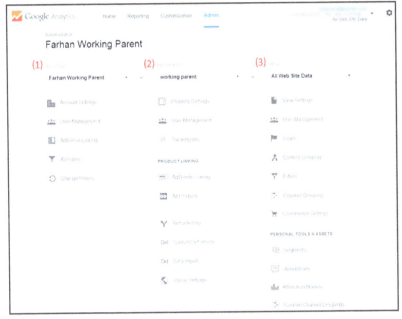

Fig 10.7 The main administration page has three main sections: 1) Account, 2) Property and 3)View settings.

You will see this the page is split into three columns with links for each that have section-specific settings.

The first column on the left (1) holds the settings for the 'Account' – that is the user details about you and other users who you want to be able to access your Google Analytics Account.

The middle column (2) has the settings for the 'Property' that is the website itself. It's here where you'll define settings for your website or websites and it's here where you will find that all-important tracking code.

Just a quick aside while we're here: clicking on the actual property drop-down list will display the different websites that you have set to the same account. In my case, I defined two websites under the same account (see Fig 10.5), so clicking on the drop-down list will display however many web properties you have associated with the account.

Fig 10.8 I can access either of my site settings directly from here, rather than jumping back to the homepage (and then having to choose the other website). Note that you can also use the drop-down menu on the first section 'Account' (1) if you have multiple accounts set up.

The third section on the right (3) is the settings for the 'View' of your analytics (according to which account and property you have previously set in columns (1) and (2)). This is where we'll be configuring two important settings in Chapter 12.

Have a look round here. The developers have gone to a lot of effort to set it out logically so that you can find settings that pertain to your main area of interest, i.e. the account, property or view level within the admin area.

In the next chapter we are going to generate the tracking code and install it onto your own blog.

Chapter 11:

Installing the tracking code on your website.

Now that you've created your account and set up the details of the blog you want to track, you need to install the tracking code onto your website. You'll do this in two steps:

1) Copy the tracking code from Google Analytics.

2) Paste the tracking code into your blog template.

     * Firstly, to get the tracking code from Google Analytics, go back to the main 'Admin' screen:

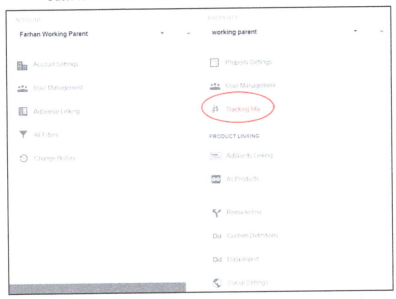

Fig11.1 Make sure you have the right property selected and then choose 'Tracking Info' from the menu.

* Clicking on 'Tracking Info' will cause that entry to expand.

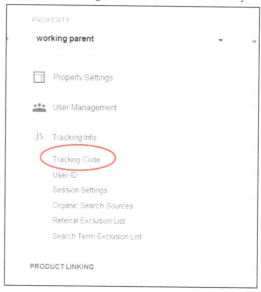

Fig 11.2 Here is where you can find the tracking code for your individual blog.

This takes you to a page with the tracking code to copy:

Fig 11.3 Copy all the code in the box, including the <script> and </script> tags.

* Click the cursor in the box, CTRL+A then CTRL+C.

If you go further down this page, you'll see a few different methods to implement the tracking code in your site, including a PHP implementation and by using Google Tag Manager. But the simplest method is to do a direct copy and paste into your site.

You'll notice that it asks you to paste this code into every page you want to track; that's quite time-consuming to do for every page. Fortunately, your blogging service has a feature in it that will allow you to paste the code directly into universal header template that goes across your whole site.

If you're using WordPress

There are a few different ways to install Google Analytics into your WordPress site. I'll show you two methods: one to insert the code directly into the site and another using a plugin. Both work equally well.

The direct implementation

Once you have the code copied from Google Analytics (see Fig 11.3), go into your WordPress admin area. Each theme will have this in a different area and generally it will be under your installed theme roll-out menu. Find the menu item that takes you to an area with a header/footer input box:

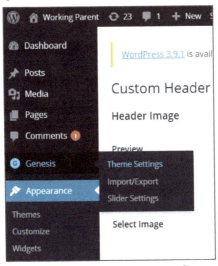

Fig 11.4 If you're using the Genesis Theme go to Genesis → Theme Settings.

* Scroll down towards the bottom to locate the header/footer scripts.

* In the first box (the 'Header and Footer Scripts') paste in the code from Google Analytics.

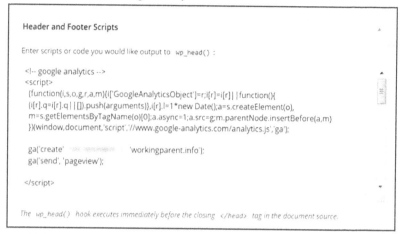

Fig 11.5 Pasting the Google Analytics code into the <head> in the theme settings will ensure that it runs site-wide. Do make sure that you hit 'Save Settings' at the bottom of the page for this to take effect.

If you use this method, bear in mind that whenever you change your theme, you will have to re-import the Google Analytics code back into your WordPress theme install.

The plugin implementation

There are lots of different plugins for Google Analytics, but basically they will do the same thing as you manually pasting the code into the theme header's file. The better plugins will do more than paste the code into the header, though. I use the Yoast SEO (Search Engine Optimisation) plugin, which amongst many other cool SEO tasks has a slot for me to pull in my Google Analytics code.

Fig 11.6 Using theYoast Google Analytics importer, which is part of theYoast SEO toolset, you can directly import your Google Analytics tracking code.

The plugin will ask you to authorise permission to access your Google Analytics account. Do this in the normal manner, sign in if you haven't already and then hit the 'Allow' button for the plugin to connect to your Google Analytics account.

Once in, a drop-down menu will appear with all your web properties available.

Fig 11.7 Expanding the Profile drop-down list will allow you to see all the Analytics properties that you have set up. Choose the appropriate one and select 'in the header (default)' in the drop-down box asking where to place the tracking code.

If you're using Blogger

If you're using Blogger, you'll find the header insertion in the Settings — Other menu item.

Fig 11.8 Use the Settings — Other menu item to insert your Google Analytics identifier code.

Here you can specify the correct tracking number, as shown at the top of Fig 11.3.

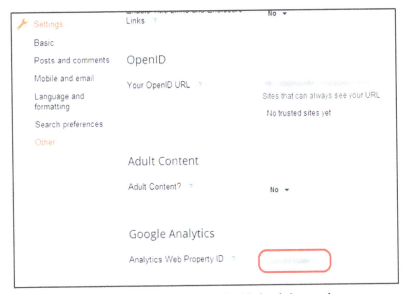

Fig 11.9 As Blogger is a Google product, you should already be signed into your Google account. All you need to do is enter the ID number (see Fig 11.3) – that's it!

Testing that your installation worked

Now that you've installed the code, you need to test that it works. Firstly you will have to wait for at least 24 hours before you can see any results, although you should immediately see that the code has made it across your website. Go to a few different pages on your site and check the source code in your browser (in Chrome and Firefox, do this by right-clicking in a blank area and selecting 'View Page Source' in the pop-up menu; in Internet Explorer, right-click and choose 'View Source').

Once in, search (CTRL+F) for your Analytics Web Property ID, should begin 'UA-'.

```
<!-- google analytics -->
<script>
  (function(i,s,o,g,r,a,m){i['GoogleAnalyticsObject']=r;i[r]=i[r]||function(){
  (i[r].q=i[r].q||[]).push(arguments)},i[r].l=1*new Date();a=s.createElement(o),
  m=s.getElementsByTagName(o)[0];a.async=1;a.src=g;m.parentNode.insertBefore(a,m)
  })(window,document,'script','//www.google-analytics.com/analytics.js','ga');

  ga('create', 'UA-                                   );
  ga('send', 'pageview');

</script>
```

Fig 11.10 Search a few pages across your site to make sure that the Analytics code is installed correctly — search using the term 'UA-' should take you to Analytics tags in the source code, if it doesn't, make sure you've saved the changes in your blogging platform and have reloaded the page in your browser (do a CTRL+F5 to make sure you're not reloading from the cache).

Congratulations, you now have Google Analytics installed on your blog!

We've walked through step-by-step how to do it and test that it is working correctly. In the next chapter we are going to learn how to exclude certain IP addresses from the results. Why do we want to do this? Well firstly we want to exclude our own IP addresses so that the analytics we get are a true reflection of visitor's activity on our site, i.e. don't include our own surfing as we continue to tinker and test changes we make. Let's dive straight in.

Chapter 12:

Creating filters to filter out your own IP address.

Before you go any further, make sure you filter out your own visits. This is especially important when you have a new blog because to start with, most of your visits will be from yourself as you establish whether your site and posts are working correctly. Filtering out your own IP address is quite simple to do.

- Go back to the main 'Admin' menu in the top left bar.
- In the right-hand 'VIEW' menu click on 'Filters'.

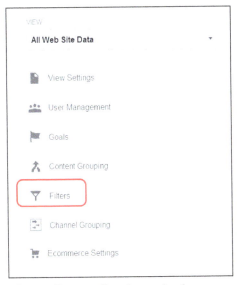

Fig 12.1 Create a filter to filter out all analytics related to your own visit.

* Press on the 'Create New Filter' button.

Fig 12.2 Create as many filters as you need, depending upon how many different machines/devices you are likely to view your blog on.You don't want to artificially inflate the number of visitors and pageviews by including your own sessions.

Typically you want to filter out the IP address your machine is linked to.

* Choose to 'Exclude' 'traffic from the IP addresses' 'that are equal to'.

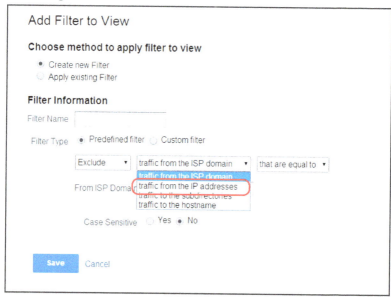

Fig 12.3 Note that your IP address could change depending upon how many times your ISP (Internet Service Provider) changes your individual IP address.

* Now find out what your IP address is by typing in, 'What's my IP?' to your favourite search engine.

Fig 12.4 Keep an eye on this, as your IP address could change. If and when it does, go back into the filter (through Admin — Filters (under the rightmost column — 'VIEW') and amend to the new IP address you are assigned.

* Go back and enter this into the area.

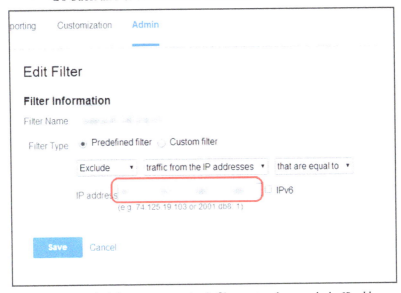

Fig 12.5 It's worthwhile setting up multiple filter names that match the IP address you are trying to filter out, e.g. home laptop, iPad, work computer.

You can see by looking through the menus that there are literally hundreds of configuration settings you can make, but now you've got the two most important tasks in the Admin area done. Now let's go on to the fun part and find out what's really going on with your site.

Part 4:

How to
analyse your data

Chapter 13:

So much data – what do I actually need to know?

Despite the best marketing efforts of the analytics platform you decide to use, don't expect the answer to be presented to you on a plate when you first open up your analytics software (sorry to be the one to burst your bubble). The opening page of your analytics is a fairly good dashboard, but don't come to rely on it for all your answers. It is a snapshot of what is happening on your site and will provide the basis of questions more than answers. I'll show you in Chapter 21 how you can create custom dashboards that will be more relevant to your blog.

You will, however, see a lot of data presented to you on your homepage dashboard.

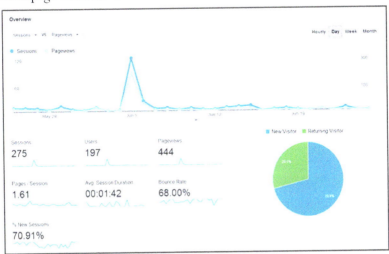

Fig 13.1 Where do I start? Are these figures good? Are these figures of any use to me?

But what exactly do all these numbers mean? How do you know if they're any good? How do you go about improving them? Which ones should you improve? Do you need to improve all of them and if so, by how much?

It's very easy to get lost before you even get started, especially when your analytics platform throws numbers at you out of the box.

Let's start with some definitions and figure out what it is that your site is trying to achieve.

Sessions – As defined by Google, a 'session' is 'the period of time a user is actively engaged with your website, app, etc.'.

What this means is how many times a visitor comes on to your website. The visitor may come once and surf three pages, may see one page and leave, may watch a video – whatever it is the visitor does, her individual visit is described as a session and she could easily come back and have another session.

275 sessions doesn't tell you much. From this figure you don't know if that was one visitor who came to your site 275 times or whether it was 275 different visitors to your site. Much like all of these figures, looking at one number in isolation is both useless and quite dangerous.

The real art of using your analytics to drive decisions about 'what to do on your blog' and 'how to measure its success and its value' is by using the numbers in combination to inform your decisions and to arrive at meaningful conclusions.

The next metric – **users** – tells you how many different people came to your site, right?

No. It tells you how many different IP addresses came to your website. Google defines users as those 'that have had at least one session within the selected date range'. You'd be forgiven for thinking that this was the unique number of people who visited your site but it is actually the unique number of IP addresses that visited your site, i.e. had a session on your site.

So what's the difference?

While the difference may be subtle it could be very significant.

- Say you visit your site on your work machine at IP address my.workplace.ip.address,

- then you go home and visit your site again at my.home.ip.address and

- finally you visit it on your tablet at a Wi-Fi-enabled coffee shop at my.tablet.ip.address.

What's happened is that even though you visited the site three times, Google Analytics will still count this as three users, even though it was you three times on different IP addresses (my.workplace.ip.address, my.home.ip.address and my.tablet.ip.address).

Consider the opposite of this example:

- You visit your blog at a computer store at computer.store.ip.address and then leave.

- Someone else comes afterwards on the same machine you've been on and surfs to your website at the same IP address computer.store.ip.address (you fiendishly set your blog to be the homepage of the browser so everyone sees it – by the way this doesn't work at the Apple store; the 'geniuses' who work there are smart to that old ruse and a lot of empirical research went into finding this out!).

Well what happens here is that you'll get two sessions but now only one user.

This is because the cookie that is dropped on the machine reads the IP address and can't distinguish between two different sets of eyeballs. So your analytics software assumes that you logged on twice, even though someone else actually viewed your page.

You may think that this brings into doubt the whole analytics framework and may make you wonder how well you can trust this technology, if at all. Well analytics platforms need ways to calculate 'things' and those 'things' have to be given names. The best way to define certain 'things' is to give them a name with a broad enough definition – here users are referred to as having 'had at least one session within the selected date range'. In the example of the computer store, the computer did have more than one session so it is counted as such.

You can never really be completely sure and no method of calculation is 100% foolproof. Consider the following:

- You log onto your site on your work machine on Day One.
- You log onto your site again on Day Two but this time show four of your work colleagues the site.

Again, the analytics shows you as one user (based on the IP address and the cookies) but really five pairs of eyeballs were looking and consuming your site (i.e. you and your four colleagues). How could any analytics platform allow for this? Obviously it can't, so it makes the best and most reasonable definition it can. What I'm trying to illustrate are the considerations around these metrics so that *you can draw additional insight into these.*

Pageviews is fairly obvious. It's the total number of pages, including repeated views of the same page in a given period, and there's little ambiguity in the definition and the way it is calculated. It doesn't matter how many people are looking at your monitor, the page only loads once, i.e. is requested once.

Pages/Session is quite simply the number of pageviews divided by the number of sessions (not users) that occurred in a given time period. What this shows is how many pages (on average) each session generated. Remember that the same user may come back in different sessions.

Average Sessions duration is the amount of time a user spent looking around your site, not the amount of time spent on a page.

The **Bounce Rate** refers to the number of people who visited your site and left after only having viewed one page – bounce rate has traditionally been taken as a hostile, negative trait.

As I briefly illustrated in Chapter 6, a bounce may be a good thing if you've designed it into a page, e.g. getting people to sign up to webinar hosted on a different site. I'll show you how to create events in Chapter 20 so that you can subtract the 'Hoorays' out and actually have the bounce show you the 'Uggghhhs'.

% New Sessions. It's important to understand that this does not mean new users. Instead, it means a new session, even if that session was set up by someone who already visited your site from a different machine or device. Google defines % New Sessions as 'an estimate of the percentage of first time visits'. You can see here how easy it is to misinterpret these metrics to mean something that they're not to meant to mean – many people do this, so if you understand these then you are already far ahead of the pack.

Next you can see the **New Visitors** versus **Returning Visitor** as a pie chart. Again, think of this loosely as a new person or someone coming back to your site – but the definition cannot be as tight as that because of the numerous edge case scenarios. Try to put these edge case scenarios out of your head at the moment and keep consistent with the definitions provided, otherwise you won't be able to move forward. A lot of very clever people have spent a lot of time thinking and coming up with these concepts. The important thing about these definitions is that they are generally accepted and so long as everyone is consistent, the various outliers will essentially level out and when you use metrics in conjunction with each other and in context, you will quickly be able to see the outliers and establish their significance.

In the next chapter we are going to find out what the differences between dimensions and metrics are in Google Analytics, and how by knowing this you can extract a tonne of valuable data about your audience, how your audience gets to your blog and how well your blog is serving that audience. This is where it really gets interesting — hold on tight!

Chapter 14:

Exploring Google Analytics.

Google Analytics is broken into several sections, which you'll find on the left menu bar:

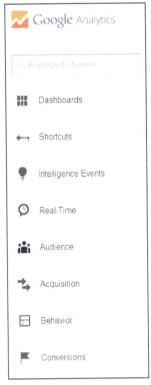

Fig 14.1 Each Analytics section expands out with section specific metrics and dimensions.

It's not my intention to be a reference manual and tell you what each of the sections do. There's already a very good reference manual and many online tutorials concerning this. **I'm far more interested in telling you how you can use these analytics to define and**

drive a successful blog. Although I will provide explanations of what each of these items mean, I will focus more on showing you how you can use these metrics and dimensions in analysing your blog. You will pick up the meanings far quicker than any instruction manual or help guide would show you.

Before we go into each section, I've mentioned 'metrics' and 'dimensions' a couple of times, so let's take a minute to define what these mean. Learning their meanings will help you to understand the whole ethos of how Google Analytics is laid out in the way it is and why particular metrics belong to certain sections and not to others.

Metrics and dimensions are so commonly misunderstood by novices and even professional analytics users (not to mention the 'experts' who will charge you two grand for a course) that a user can waste endless time hunting for a number in a section in which it will never appear and never understand why they can't find it. Or a user may see a metric once and then never know how to go back and find that metric again.

In the most basic sense:

- A 'dimension' is something that can be described or given a name.
- A 'metric' is the measure of a particular attribute of that dimension.

Seems a bit abstract?

Let's look at examples. I generally believe that examples are the best way to understand abstract concepts – that's why I use them a lot.

- A dimension could be a city, like 'London', 'New York' or 'Paris'.
- A corresponding metric could be:
    * 'population'
    * 'area in square miles'
    * 'average temperature'
    * 'happiness coefficient'

Let's step through how we ourselves would construct dimensions and metrics. From this you'll be able to understand how and why Google Analytics is structured the way it is and even more importantly, you will be able to find the data you are after a lot faster and make your reports far richer.

Let's look at the climate guide for a couple of fictional planets.

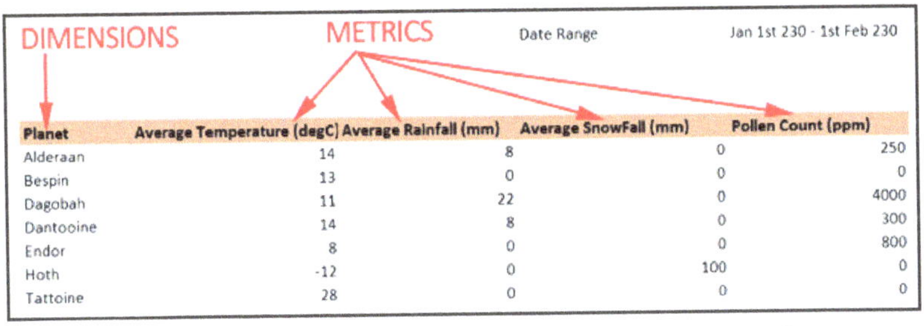

Planet	Average Temperature (degC)	Average Rainfall (mm)	Average SnowFall (mm)	Pollen Count (ppm)
Alderaan	14	8	0	250
Bespin	13	0	0	0
Dagobah	11	22	0	4000
Dantooine	14	8	0	300
Endor	8	0	0	800
Hoth	-12	0	100	0
Tattoine	28	0	0	0

DIMENSIONS   METRICS   Date Range   Jan 1st 230 - 1st Feb 230

Fig 14.2 Climate guide of a series of planets (I made the numbers up, before anyone asks!).

You can see here the difference between dimensions and metrics.

- The dimension is the name of the planet you are measuring.

- The metric is the individual number for temperature, rainfall, snowfall and pollen count.

Note also that in the top right corner is a date range. If you were to look up a different date range, say June 540, all the metrics would change to reflect the figures for that time period. The dimensions would, however, stay the same (unless of course a planet happened to be destroyed).

So what would you call this table? You'd probably give it a name like 'Climate Guide' and maybe stick it in a section containing other tables relating to the planet itself. That section (which you may want to name 'Planet Data') may have a structure of tables like this:

- Planet Data
    * Planet Climate Guide (table)
        ▪ Planet (dimension)
            ▪ Average temperature (metric)

- Average rainfall (metric)
- Average snowfall (metric)
- Average pollen count (metric)
* Planet Demographics (table)
  - Planet (dimension)
    - Population (metric)
    - Population density (metric)
    - Species living there (metric)
    - Male/female ratio (metric)
* Planet Quality of Life Guide (table)
  - Planet (dimension)
    - Employment rate (metric)
    - Rebel employment rate (metric)
    - Imperial forces employment rate (metric)
    - Crime rate (metric)
    - Happiness coefficient (metric)
    - Rebel to Imperial conflict ratio (metric)
    - Jedi schools density (metric)

Say now you want to include more data about this universe, you could have different sections like 'people', 'vehicles', 'weapons' and so on. Let's look at our sections now.

- Planet data
- People data
- Vehicle data
- Weapon data

You can see that they all hold different dimensions and different metrics. For instance, you couldn't have data about rainfall and which ship can do the Kessel run in under twelve parsecs in direct comparison – those pieces of data don't fit together because they don't have the same dimensions. Yet you will still find experienced analytics users trying to find different data types in one place, like pageviews and average sessions duration and asking how the two are related.

This is why it's so important to understand this concept and I hope the example above has helped you to understand how different sections contain different tables and how these different tables have metrics that relate to certain types of dimensions.

You can also understand how a set of metrics in one table doesn't relate to a set of metrics in another section's tables (in the same way that the 'firing rate of a standard issue Imperial blaster' has nothing to do with the 'temperature on planet Dagobah').

The problem arises when you go into your analytics platform expecting disparate terms to relate, i.e. trying to relate user metrics and site-related metrics in one. Knowing the areas that are relatable in Google Analytics and why they belong together will save you a lot of time and effort.

You can, of course, put unrelated data into a dashboard where it might be useful, and I'll show you how to do this in Chapter 21. For now I want to continue our tour de force of the how Google Analytics is split into different sections and where you can find the data you need.

Chapter 15:

Google Analytics audience data.

Let's dive right in now to see where all your lovely data lives in Google Analytics.

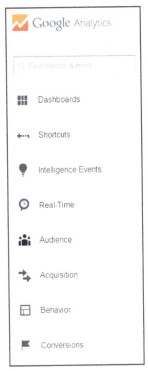

Fig 15.1 The left side menu bar is the main navigation panel. Each of these sections expands to give finer detail.

We're actually going to start half-way down this list at 'Audience' and work downwards from here. Why? Well this is how you will be using Google Analytics on a day-to-day basis.

For completeness, I'll very quickly explain what the top menu items do.

- The topmost menu option (called 'Dashboards') is where you'll create your own dashboards that you can share with potential advertisers (see Chapter 21).

- 'Shortcuts', as the name suggests, is where you can create shortcuts to various custom tables which we are about to create.

- 'Intelligence Events' is where you are going to create and record events based on your own website's behaviour (see Chapter 20).

- 'Realtime' is where you can see exactly what is happening on your site at that precise moment. This is quite useful to see how a campaign is performing in real-time.

But as I mentioned, your day-to-day journey is going to start at the 'Audience' level and it's here where you'll be able to see:

- who is visiting your website;

- where geographically they are coming from;

- which browsers and OS visitors are using to browse your site;

- what devices (phones, tablets, desktops) visitors use to access your site

- and how visitors flow through your site.

Fig 15.2 Clicking on any of the left menu bar headings will expand the menu to display the different areas within.

Fig 15.3 The first item that you will see is the 'Overview' menu item.

Clicking on 'Overview' gives you top-level headlines about your audience. Here you'll be shown:

- How many 'Sessions' your blog had – a session is defined as a period of time a visitor is actively engaged with you site or app.

- How many 'Users' have visited your site – a user defined as someone who has had at least one session on your site.

- 'Pageviews' is fairly self-explanatory, but the key thing is to see how many 'Pageviews' those users and sessions have generated (the next metric directly helps you with this).

- 'Pages/Session' – is 'Pageviews' divided by 'Sessions'. This is important to know, as you can see how actively people are engaging with your site, i.e. how many pages on average are viewed in a single session.

- 'Avg. Session Duration' – shows the time that a user spends on your site. Essentially Google Analytics records the time a user lands on your site, and each subsequent action is then time-stamped until all actions have finished (either someone leaves your site or is inactive for 30 minutes). After 30 minutes of inactivity, the recording of activity ends and all data is logged as a session. If the user engages again after 30 minutes than any new data is counted as a new session.

- 'Bounce Rate' is defined as the percentage of sessions that only had one pageview. This is often thought to be a bad thing, as the prevalent feeling is that the user came to your site, didn't like what she saw and left. However, as we have seen, that sometimes that may not be the case. I'll show you in Chapter 20 how you can define events to show which bounces actually triggered an event and how to exclude those events from your 'Bounce Rate' calculation.

- '% New Sessions' shows you how many new sessions occurred on your site. It's very easy to get confused and assume that this means how many new people visited the site. The distinction is that a new session could be the same person revisiting your site, perhaps because his first session was on his work PC and the new session on his home PC or via a mobile device.

By expanding the 'Geo' tab, you can start to see where your visitors are currently located.

Fig 15.4 The 'Audience | Location' menu answers questions about where your traffic is coming from.

This view will present you with lots of useful metrics based upon groups of people from a certain geographical location. Don't get this confused with individuals from various countries; the table displays what is known as 'aggregated' data (i.e. the metrics in here will tell you how groups of visitors from these countries behave).

Common table functionality and secondary dimensions

Before we dive into the various intelligence data you can gain from this report, now is a good place to see what the buttons and menu items at the head of of table actually do. You'll be able to use this functionality regardless of which view you are in.

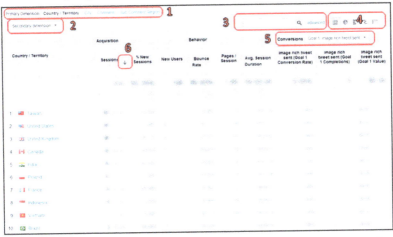

Fig 15.5 There are a number of extra attributes you can bring into any reports and many ways in which you can arrange the data to ask and answer whatever questions you have of it.

At this particular point, I want to focus on the functionality of the table rather than what the definitions mean (they're fairly self-explanatory and you can look them up by hovering the mouse over each one). After all, this book aims to give you more ways to find insight rather than being a plain instruction manual.

I've highlighted six areas to show you how you can customise the default layout to suit your own purposes.

1) Changing the 'Primary dimension' – As this screen grab was taken in the 'Geo' section, all the primary dimensions relate to 'Geo'. This area allows you to quickly switch your primary dimension based on the section, i.e. you can order by city, continent and sub-continent. As you move around different areas of the analytics

platform, you'll see that the alternative primary dimensions will change according to the context.

For example, if we were to look at the alternative primary dimensions for type of mobile devices, we'd see an alternative set of primary dimensions based on this context:

Fig 15.6 The 'Primary Dimension' list updates according to what section you are viewing (from the left side menu).

2) The 'Secondary dimension' is also a powerful way to customise your analytics to answer questions that are specific to your site.

This works by taking your primary dimension and then breaking that query down into specific data sets. Sounds a bit complex? Let's look at an example to simplify things.

Keeping geographic view as our primary dimension, let's say we want to know which social network people from specific countries have come from. In this case, we would select the secondary dimension and choose 'Social Network' from the drop-down menu, as follows:

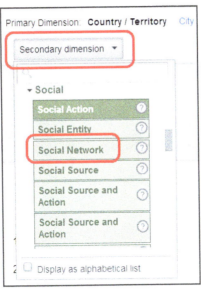

Fig 15.7 The 'Primary dimension' will now be filtered based on the selected 'Secondary dimension'. In this case, we'll see different countries filtered by the social network that brought visitors to your website.

Fig 15.8 Now we can see visitor analytics per country based on the social network that initially brought them to the site.

In fact, when the secondary dimension (2) is combined with the advanced filter (3), you can fine-tune the question to precisely hone in on what you are looking for.

3) Using the 'advanced' filter option, we can now single in on metrics based on either of the dimensions (primary or secondary) that we've specified.

Fig 15.9 Clicking on the 'advanced' filter option, a new input area will open where you can specify any combination of dimensions from either your primary dimension (1) or secondary dimension (2).

This is what is known as a procedure with an argument. The procedure in this case is the 'Include' (A), the remainder (to the right) is the argument, which is basically a way to specify something.

For instance, 'Please get me an ice cream with strawberry sauce in a cone,' is a series of instructions based on differing conditions. If we were to write this as a procedure, it would look like this: 'getIceCream(topping, holder)'. Populating the procedure with the arguments 'strawberry sauce' and 'cone' the procedure would then look like getIceCream('strawberry sauce', 'cone').

When you go into the 'advanced' filter, you can construct your arguments in four parts to specify the exact dimensions you are interested in. Google Analytics provides a very simple way to do this with drop-down menus.

Section A lets you 'Include' or 'Exclude' the argument:

Fig 15.10 Choose to 'Include' or 'Exclude' the argument you are about to build into the results table.

Section B lets you specify either your primary or secondary dimension or a set of default dimensions that are relevant to either the primary or secondary dimensions that you chose:

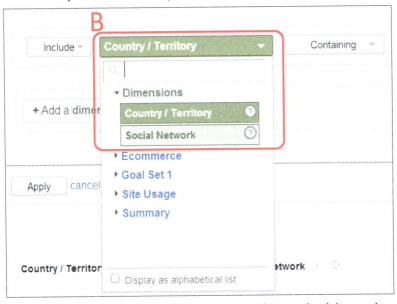

Fig 15.11 In this case, the primary dimension 'Country / Territory' and the secondary dimension 'Social Network' are the two dimensions that appear in our drop-down menu.Whichever different primary and secondary dimensions ((1) and (2) from Fig 15.5) you choose will appear in this drop-down menu.

Section C lets you determine how to choose between (B) based on the next part (D):

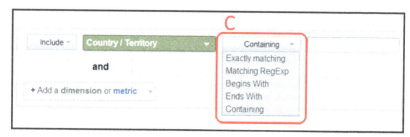

Fig 15.12 *This box gives you the functionality to separate terms (see (D) below) in your dimensions that would otherwise be very difficult to analyse individually.*

Section D is where you type in the thing that you are interested in:

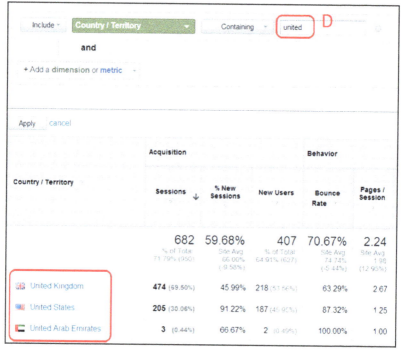

Fig 15.13 *Here you can see countries containing the term 'United' brings up results for 'United Kingdom', 'United States' and 'United Arab Emirates'.*

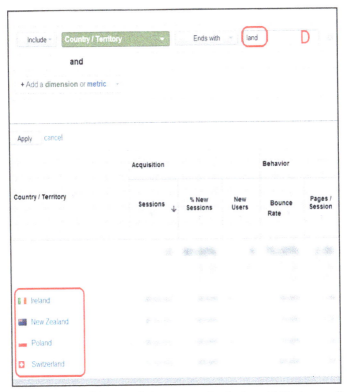

Fig 15.14 Setting the filter to include countries that 'ends with' (C) the term 'land' pulls up results for 'Ireland', 'New Zealand', 'Poland' and 'Switzerland'.

Over in this area, you will find five different ways to lay out your data table:

Fig 15.15 The five different options to lay out the data are E) table format (default), F) pie chart G) as a horizontal bar graph, H) as a comparison bar graph (horizontal), and I) as a pivot table.

You've already seen Layout E, in the above figures and in fact, this is the default layout that Google Analytics gives you. Let's take a look at the others.

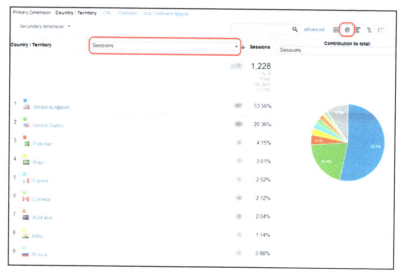

Fig 15.16 Layout F displays the same information but visualised as a pie chart.

Notice the drop-down list at the top of the second column. Here you can sort along all the same column headers as in the default view; the figures and the graph will update.

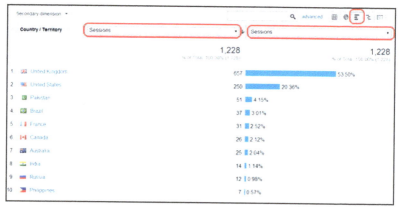

Fig 15.17 The bar chart option lays out your data in two side-by-side columns.

The really clever thing with this report is that you'll notice that at the top of the two columns (highlighted with the red border) there are two drop-down lists. This is a really powerful feature, enabling you to compare different metric headers against each other. In the figure above (Fig 15.17), you'll notice that both menus arc displaying 'Sessions' and that both totals are 1,228 sessions.

Expand one of the drop-down menus and you'll see that you have access to all the metric headers driven by your primary (and secondary) dimensions:

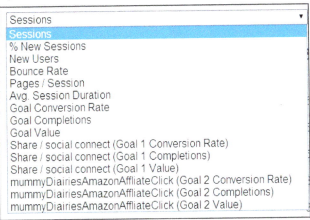

Fig 15.18 *You can define the data you want charted by making a selection in the drop-down menu.*

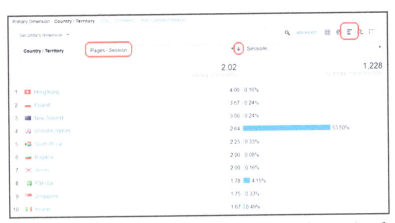

Fig 15.19 *You can plot the first set of metrics based on the order of the second set of metrics.*

In this case, I've chosen the middle column to display 'Pages / Session' metric and the right side column to display the 'Sessions' metric (the left-side column displays the dimensions). Using this data, I can see that although visitors in Hong Kong are the most engaged (i.e. consume the most amount of pages in each session), the overall traffic is very low as a percentage of the total traffic.

I can also see that visitors from my highest traffic area are consuming an above average pages/session, i.e. 2.64 pages per session versus the average of 2.02 listed at the header of the middle column. Strategies based on this analysis will tell you in which countries you have an under-served audience. In this example visitors from 'Hong Kong', 'Poland' and 'New Zealand' are very engaged but in small numbers. Some local SEO for these countries or engagement with influencers in these territories would be one way to drive more visits from those locations.

Typically you will need two metrics to compare against each other, and this is a very cool and quick way to simplify and hone in on the data you need.

Note: I can also order the data by clicking on the downward-pointing arrow to change from ascending (smallest to biggest) to descending (biggest to smallest).

Fig 15.20 The fourth visualisation type is the comparison view (D).

In the right-side column you can see which dimensions are above and which are below the site average session duration.

- The vertical line is the average

- Any bars to the right will be in green are above average.
- Any to the left in red are below your site average.

This is absolutely invaluable when proving to an advertiser that you have an audience in a particular location and in Chapter 21 I'll show you how to collate all these into a single-view dashboard.

The same applies with changing and mixing the metrics from the drop-down menus, as I mentioned in Part G.

Fig 15.21 You can use the drop-down menu lists to chart one metric against another and see how comparatively well each country (dimension) performs against each other. At any point, you can also change or add a secondary dimension, e.g. use 'Social Network' instead of 'Country'.

The last button would convert the table into a pivot table:

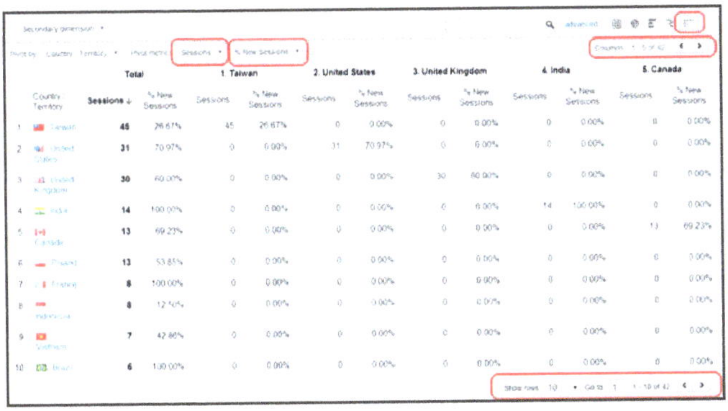

Fig 15.22 The same metrics are available in the pivot tables, depending upon how you want to lay out your data.

To move across the columns, use the arrow navigation buttons at the upper right and to move up and down the rows, use the navigation buttons at the bottom right. You can add in secondary dimensions as you please.

4) The last thing I want to show you is the 'Sort' button.

	Country / Territory	Acquisition			Behavior			
		Sessions ↓	% New Sessions	New Users	Bounce Rate	Pages / Session	Avg. Session Duration	
		643 % of Total 100.00% (643)	59.72% Site Avg 59.72% (0.00%)	384 % of Total 100.00% (384)	56.77% Site Avg 56.77% (0.00%)	4.08 Site Avg 4.08 (0.00%)	00:06:19 Site Avg 00:06:19 (0.00%)	
1	United Kingdom	214 (33.28%)	42.52%	91 (23.70%)	37.38%	8.22	00 14 50	
2	United States	79 (12.29%)	69.62%	55 (14.32%)	69.62%	1.47	00 01 12	
3	Taiwan	46 (7.15%)	28.26%	13 (3.39%)	76.09%	1.33	00 01 43	
4	Canada	28 (4.35%)	78.57%	22 (5.73%)	75.00%	1.68	00 02 05	
5	India	27 (4.20%)	88.89%	24 (6.25%)	51.85%	1.74	00 02 19	
6	Poland	18 (2.80%)	61.11%	11 (2.86%)	66.67%	1.83	00 01 57	
7	Pakistan	16 (2.49%)	43.75%	7 (1.82%)	43.75%	2.00	00 03 21	

Fig 15.23 Here you can see that we are sorting in descending order for sessions, i.e. from most sessions to least amount of sessions.

To change the order, just click on the arrow again and you'll sort in ascending order. To order by any of the other metrics, all you need to do is click on their title and the table will be sorted according to your new selection.

Country / Territory	Acquisition			Behavior		
	Sessions	% New Sessions	New Users	Bounce Rate	Pages / Session	Avg. Session Duration
	643	59.72%	384	56.77%	4.08	00:06:19
1 Belgium	14	28.57%	4	14.29%	12.07	00:12:51
2 Venezuela	2	50.00%	1	50.00%	10.00	00:10:10
3 United Kingdom	214	42.52%	91	37.38%	8.22	00:14:50
4 Ghana	1	100.00%	1	0.00%	7.00	00:22:47
5 Romania	2	100.00%	2	0.00%	5.50	00:02:30
6 Greece	2	100.00%	2	0.00%	3.50	00:03:23
7 South Korea	1	100.00%	1	0.00%	3.00	00:01:28
8 Vietnam	7	42.86%	3	85.71%	3.00	00:01:06
9 Turkey	3	100.00%	3	33.33%	2.67	00:01:08
10 Hungary	4	75.00%	3	25.00%	2.50	00:00:35

Fig 15.24 By clicking on the pages/session header, I can now order my data in terms of highest to lowest 'Pages/Session'.

Behaviour, Technology and Mobile

The next three sections tell you about the behaviour, the technology visitors use to consume your blog and the split between mobile and desktop usage.

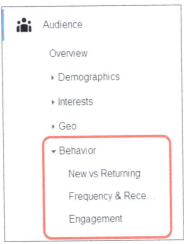

Fig 15.25 The behaviour menu has three sections i) 'New vs Returning' visitors ii) 'Frequency & Recency' and iii) 'Engagement' metrics.

The 'New vs Returning' menu will give you comparative metrics on how your new visitors compare with your returning visitors.

'New vs Returning' visitors has always caused a lot of contention when I've been in digital strategy meetings because no one really knows how to define what a successful measure of this should be. Let's consider the following scenario and see how it plays out:

New visitors 80%

Returning visitors 20%

Is this good or bad?

The answer could be good (you are getting a lot of new visitors to the site so your SEO, PPC or social media campaigns must be doing really well) or bad (all these new visitors are coming to your site once and choosing not to return).

As with so many things, the answer really depends on what you are trying to achieve.

Is your site a one-hit site, i.e. a site where your audience can get everything from you in one session? If your aim is purely to refer them to a sign-up form, then once they've signed up to the offer, your site has done its job and there's no reason for that visitor to return. Then again, perhaps you're relying on return visits to generate more money through banner advertising.

Whatever your aim, it's unlikely that you are going to find the answer in a single metric like this one. What this report does more effectively is to show you comparisons between the behaviour of new and returning visitors.

User Type	Acquisition			Behavior		
	Sessions ↓	% New Sessions	New Users	Bounce Rate	Pages / Session	Avg. Session Duration
	643 % of Total: 100.00% (643)	59.72% Site Avg: 59.72% (0.00%)	384 % of Total: 100.00% (384)	56.77% Site Avg: 56.77% (0.00%)	4.08 Site Avg 4.08 (0.00%)	00:06:19 Site Avg 00:06:19 (0.00%)
1. New Visitor	384 (59.72%)	100.00%	384 (100.00%)	63.80%	2.40	00:02:33
2. Returning Visitor	259 (40.28%)	0.00%	0 (0.00%)	46.33%	6.57	00:11:55

Fig 15.26 You can use any of the secondary dimensions available and all the sorting options we've spoken about above.

You can see from the table above that you can compare new and returning visitors' behaviour through such metrics as 'Bounce Rate', 'Pages/Session' and 'Average Session Duration'. This gives you a much better picture of engagement. From Fig 15.26 we can see that the 'Returning Visitors', although in the minority, are twice as engaged as the 'New Visitors' (by looking at the 6.57 'Pages/Session' they view compared to the 2.4 'Pages/Session' viewed by new visitors). This shows that your 'Returning Visitors' really like your content. Whatever channels these 'New Visitors' have been acquired from (e.g. SEO, social media, AdWords), they are not yet as engaged with the blog as those who are choosing to return. Looking at this data would therefore lead you to review your acquisition strategy – is it meeting the expectation of the new audience and are you being successful in targeting them (in 'Sessions' generated, 'Pages/Session' and 'Avg. Session Duration')?

To gain deeper insights into the factors behind the behaviour, you will invariably need to add a second dimension.

The second item is about 'Frequency & Recency', which is split into two tabs:

- Count of Sessions – how many people had 'X' amount of sessions.

- Days since Last Session – how often people come back to your blog.

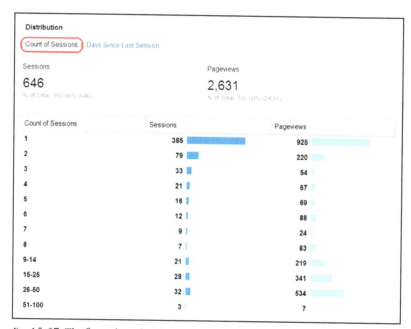

Fig 15.27 *The first tab in the 'Frequency & Recency' menu is 'Count of Sessions',
which tells us that there were 385 single session (in which a total of 925 pageviews
occurred), that there were 79 sessions consisting of 2 sessions (we'll take it that 79
people came back for a second session) and so on within the timeframe specified.*

Distribution		
Count of Sessions	Days Since Last Session	

Sessions	Pageviews
646	2,631
% of Total: 100.00% (646)	% of Total: 100.00% (2,631)

Days Since Last Session	Sessions	Pageviews
0	547	2,151
1	26	239
2	20	106
3	9	20
4	6	6
5	2	16
6	4	5
7	8	31
8-14	15	36
15-30	8	18
31-60	1	3

Fig 15.28 The second tab 'Days Since Last Session' is a bit easier to read and understand. Note that here there's no option to add in secondary dimensions.

The next two sections deal with the technology and mobile devices the visitor used to access your blog. The technology tells you which browser and operating system people are viewing your blog on and the mobile section tells you about the mobile devices people are using.

Fig 15.29 'Technology' and 'Mobile' tell you 'how' visitors are accessing your site.

Really the only actionable thing you are going to find out from here is the proportion of your audience who are viewing your blog on a mobile device (phone or tablet). This will affect the way you layout your blog, and in particular where to place your banner ads. We're going to cover a lot more of this in Chapter 22. For now, have a poke around in here to see the completeness of the reports. If knowing the browser and OS are of interest to you, you will find the answers here.

Users Flow

The final option in the 'Audience' menu is the 'Users Flow', which is one of the most intriguing ones to look at.

Fig 15.30 The last item in the 'Audience' section will map out user journeys through your blog.

Fig 15.31 The 'Users Flow' view presents a graphical layout of the paths that your visitors have collectively taken through your blog.

This is a great feature of Google Analytics because now you can see paths people are taking through your blog. I've highlighted key areas, which will quickly help you understand how this feature works.

A   This is the navigation bar. The '+' and '−' buttons scale into and out of the map (just like the scaling feature on Google maps), the left and right arrows in the circle will move you across the visualisation (as you move to the right you will note there is a '+ Step' button to add another layer of flow) and the 'Home' icon in the circle will bring you back to the home (initial) view once you've finished navigating through the menu.

B   This is where you define your primary dimension (as you would in any of the other views). Expanding it will list the primary dimensions available to you.

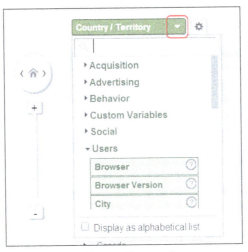

Fig 15.32 Clicking on the expand button (downward-pointing triangle) will give you a drop-down with the full list of primary dimensions to choose from.

There are so many interesting dimensions to define the flow of your data. By default, it will display Country/Territory, but if you are using social networks, SEO or PPC campaigns you can switch your primary dimension to compare how groups of different people from those channels behave.

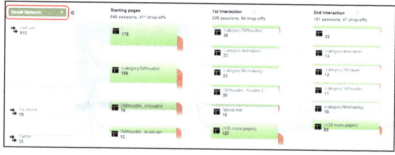

Fig 15.33 Changing the primary dimension to 'Social Network' (Social | Social Network) gives an overview of the split between (in this case) Facebook, Twitter and those who didn't arrive through a social network.

Choosing a primary dimension like this will help you to evaluate your efforts in promoting your blog. We all know that more effort and energy is expended promoting a blog than actually creating content, so this information is invaluable for you to know where to focus your marketing effort, since you will be able to see both the audience size that comes through a particular social network and also the engagement that those visitors have. I'll show you in parts 'F' and 'H' a superb way to isolate the visitors from these networks.

C   Here you can customise your dimension items, and the same rules apply in terms of dimension layout.

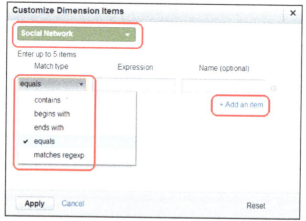

Fig 15.34 Customise your primary dimension and use a combination of expression types to fine-tune the 'User Flow' you are interested in.

For example, here I want to see how the visitors from Facebook flow through my site:

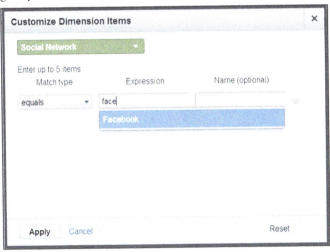

Fig 15.35 Use the autocomplete feature to populate the expression field with valid entries.

- Select 'Social | Social Network' from the top green drop-down box.

- Click on the '+ Add an item' link on the right under the name field (hidden beneath the autocomplete in this screen grab).

- With the match type set to 'equals', start typing in 'Facebook' in the expression box. You'll see that it will let you autocomplete.

- Hit the 'Apply' button.

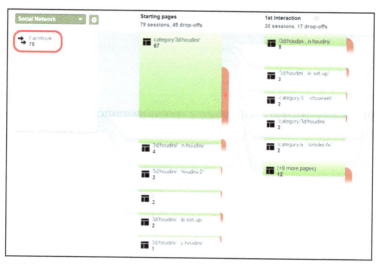

Fig 15.36 Now you can see the user flow for visitors who came through Facebook or any other referral path you specify.

D   This column shows you which pages visitors started from. Think of it as the equivalent of a landing page. I'll show you in Chapter 17 how you can tag your campaigns up so that you can refer to them in your primary dimension (Step C above). This way you can measure the effectiveness of your landing page to convert visitors through a process of steps. The column header will show you how many sessions occurred on the starting page and how many 'drop-offs', i.e. those that bounced. Note that the 'drop-offs' listed in subsequent columns are not bounces, as bounces only occur on the landing page

E   This column shows the next page that users visited in their journey. Again you can see the sessions that occurred and how many sessions ended in drop-offs. The second, third and subsequent interactions are found on the columns further right.

F   There are two special features of the boxes themselves. Firstly, just by putting the cursor over the box you will be able to find out just how much of the traffic a particular page took and how much of that individual page's traffic dropped off.

Fig 15.37 Placing the mouse pointer over an individual page will pop up that page's proportion of the total traffic and how many sessions dropped off on that page.

The second thing that you can do is to pull up a context-sensitive menu by left-clicking:

Fig 15.38 Left-click on the page's box to see a context-sensitive menu. Remember that this is all in a web browser so right-clicking would bring up your web browser's own context-sensitive menu.

Here you have three very powerful ways in which to analyse the flow through your pages. Let's step through them individually.

→ 'Highlight traffic through here' – this highlights the traffic that passes through a particular page and will fade out the rest of the visualisation.

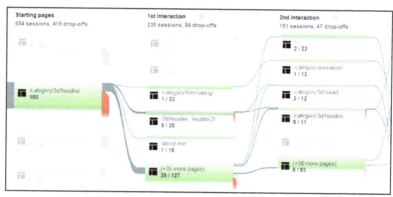

Fig 15.39 By 'highlighting', the rest of the visualisation is faded out, putting your currently selected page's traffic into context against the total blog traffic.

→ 'Explore traffic through here' – this will make the non-connected page nodes disappear from the visualisation.

Fig 15.40 Choosing to 'Explore traffic' through this page's node, will place your page in the centre of the screen with incoming pages and their traffic levels to the left and outgoing page's traffic to the right. You can add additional steps by clicking on the '+ Step' button links on either side of the visualisation – this is useful to see in greater detail what happened through a particular path, although you will lose the bigger picture (as in Fig 15.39).

This view is great when you want to see which pages/posts on your own blog are driving visitors to the page you're interested in, and you may be surprised to find that some unexpected pages/posts are driving traffic to this page. It also serves to show how well pages/ posts that you expected to drive traffic to this page actually convert.

→ 'Group details' – you can find out more information about the group's details here.

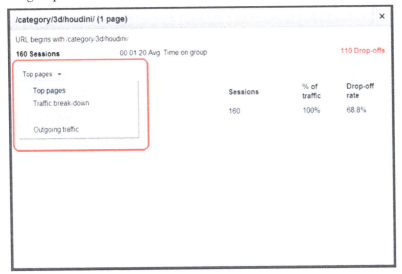

Fig 15.41 *There are different ways in which you can break down the details of the page's group.*

The 'Top pages' view shows your currently selected group of pages:

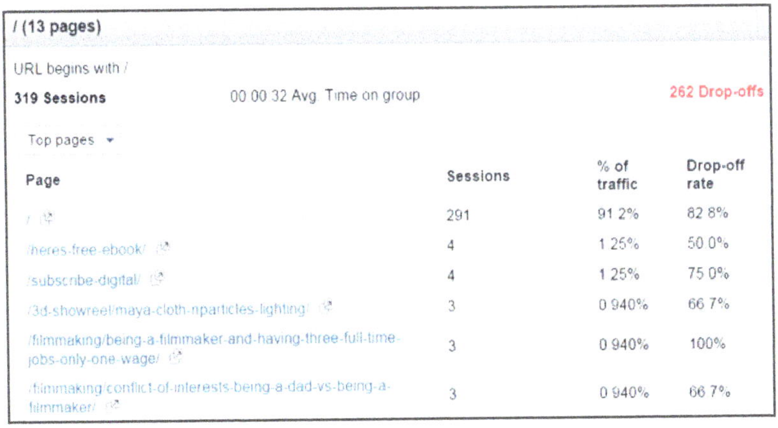

Fig 15.42 *You will see a window showing you the relative metrics from whichever step you select 'Group details' on and then 'Top Pages'. Note that these figures are relative to the primary dimension and the step number from which you execute this feature.*

The 'Traffic break-down' view will show you this individual page's geographic traffic:

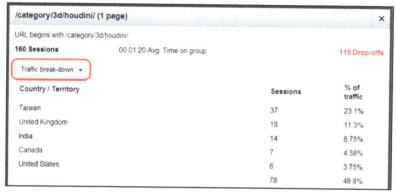

Fig 15.43 The traffic breakdown shows the traffic for the individual page (node) selected – the '% of traffic' show you that individual page's % of traffic, again remember that it is relative to the primary dimension you selected. For instance, if your primary dimension was 'Social Network' then the above table would have your social networks listed in the left column.

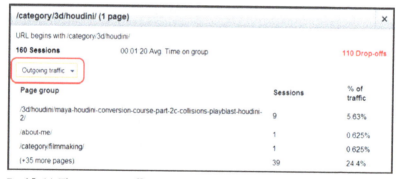

Fig 15.44 The outgoing traffic report shows where (i.e. which pages) traffic from your current page flows out to.

G   Hovering over the red area will show you the drop-off rate for an individual page.

/category/3d/houdini/
160

110   drop-offs
16.8% of total traffic

Fig 15.45 Hovering over the red box brings up its statistics and clicking on the red bar highlights all the paths that led to a drop-off on the page.

H   Clicking on any of the bottom page boxes (which say '+XX' more pages) will only bring up one menu option – the 'Group details'.

Fig 15.46 As there are multiple pages (in this case over 35), it's impossible to 'highlight' or 'explore' the traffic through all the pages.

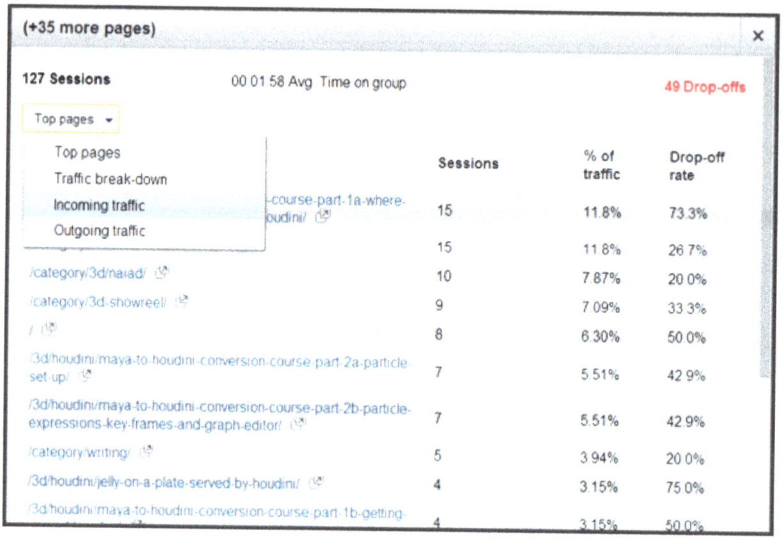

Top pages ▾				
Top pages		Sessions	% of traffic	Drop-off rate
Traffic break-down				
Incoming traffic	-course-part-1a-where-oudini/ ⊕	15	11.8%	73.3%
Outgoing traffic				
		15	11.8%	26.7%
/category/3d/naiad/ ⊕		10	7.87%	20.0%
/category/3d-showreel/ ⊕		9	7.09%	33.3%
/ ⊕		8	6.30%	50.0%
/3d/houdini/maya-to-houdini-conversion-course-part-2a-particle-set-up/ ⊕		7	5.51%	42.9%
/3d/houdini/maya-to-houdini-conversion-course-part-2b-particle-expressions-key-frames-and-graph-editor/ ⊕		7	5.51%	42.9%
/category/writing/ ⊕		5	3.94%	20.0%
/3d/houdini/jelly-on-a-plate-served-by-houdini/ ⊕		4	3.15%	75.0%
/3d/houdini/maya-to-houdini-conversion-course-part-1b-getting-		4	3.15%	50.0%

127 Sessions   00 01 58 Avg Time on group   **49 Drop-offs**

(+35 more pages)   ✕

Fig 15.47 In the first, second and subsequent 'Interaction' columns, you also have the option to view the incoming traffic to the page node you have selected.

This concludes our section on learning about your audience. In the next chapter we are going to look at how you acquire your traffic and we will learn how you can define and measure the success of a campaign and learn a great deal about your SEO (Search Engine Optimisation) efforts.

Chapter 16:

Acquisition and how to measure your effort's success.

In this chapter we are going to learn how you can measure the success of your various campaigns to attract visitors to your blog, what your best method of bringing visitors to your blog is and how you can measure the engagement of the different groups of visitors you are working so hard to get.

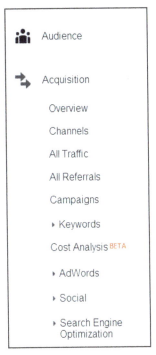

Fig 16.1 The 'Acquisition' menu lives below the 'Audience' menu.

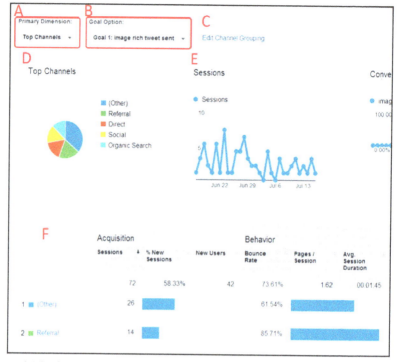

Fig 16.2 The Acquisition 'Overview' pane summarises the sources of your traffic.

Let's break this down into its component sections.

A   You can define your primary dimension in much the same
way as we've seen in the 'Audience' section, except of course
in this case your primary dimensions relate to the context
you're searching in, i.e. dimensions relating specifically to
'Acquisition'.

Fig 16.3 The primary dimensions available here all relate to 'Acquisition' dimensions.

B   Here you can choose which goal you would like to display.

C   The 'Edit Channel Grouping' link allows you to define the
     order in which you want the channels to be ordered and also
     to add your own custom channels.

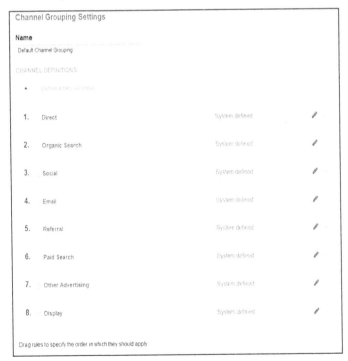

Fig 16.4 Clicking on the 'Edit Channel Grouping' takes you to the admin area where

you can add your own channel definition at the top and reorder the default layout of the channels. This is useful if you are targeting a specific channel or if a specific channel is more important to you than others. You can then define your own ranking by clicking on the left side of any of the bars and dragging them to the position you require.

D   This shows the split between your channels. Remember of course that you have the flexibility to change the order as in C above if the way Google has laid it out doesn't fit your criteria.

E   The sessions are laid out in the same way you would expect to see them in the 'Audience' layout.

F   Here's where your dimensions and metrics are laid out as they relate to acquisitions.

Now we have the overview, let's step through each of these in more detail to find out what they mean and more importantly how you can make effective use of them.

The second entry in 'Acquisition' contains details about the 'Channels' that have brought visitors to your blog:

Default Channel Grouping	Acquisition			Behavior		
	Sessions ↓	% New Sessions	New Users	Bounce Rate	Pages / Session	Avg. Session Duration
	648 % of Total 100.00% (648)	**60.19%** Site Avg 60.19% (0.00%)	**390** % of Total 100.00% (390)	**57.87%** Site Avg 57.87% (0.00%)	**3.94** Site Avg 3.94 (0.00%)	**00:05:58** Site Avg 00:05:58 (0.00%)
1 (Other)	**206** (31.79%)	55.34%	114 (29.23%)	66.02%	2.90	00:05:36
2 Direct	**190** (29.32%)	54.74%	104 (26.67%)	49.47%	6.36	00:09:44
3 Social	**135** (20.83%)	68.89%	93 (23.85%)	58.52%	1.91	00:01:46
4 Referral	**61** (9.41%)	93.44%	57 (14.62%)	80.33%	1.36	00:00:46
5 Organic Search	**56** (8.64%)	39.29%	22 (5.64%)	30.36%	7.29	00:10:13

Fig 16.5 The 'Channels' pane is similar to those seen in the 'Audience' section. It

has a graph over time in the top half and a table in the lower half – all the same functionality that we've seen in Fig 15.5 exists in these layouts.

Although the overall layout is the same as we've detailed in previous sections, there are two parts of the table I want to draw your attention to:

A   The default channel grouping shows how traffic came to your blog:

   *   Other – Although you may think that this is a collection of acquisition methods that aren't defined in the descriptions below, it can also include sources that (for whatever reason) weren't classified in one of the other four channels. In this case, 'Other' contains sessions for LinkedIn and Twitter; simply click on it to see what it contains.

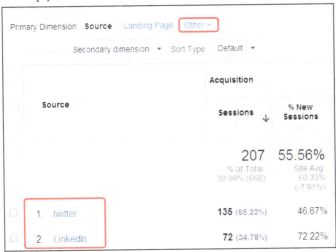

Fig 16.6 Don't assume that 'Other' doesn't contain any of the channels listed elsewhere. In this case, 'Other' refers to two social networks that you'd expect to see in another dimension (see below). If this happens to you, you can group 'Other' and 'Social Network' together by using the advanced filter that I showed you in Chapter 15.

   *   Direct – This refers to people who typed your URL into their browser, came from a favourite or had the blog thumbnail display as one of the suggested sites when they opened a new

117

tab in their browser. In some cases, it might be those who were already on your blog but were inactive for over half an hour (Google Analytics counts inactivity of half an hour as the end of the session, and in this case may explain why there are some fairly obscure URLs in the list, ones that are highly unlikely to have been manually entered into a browser).

Landing Page		Acquisition	
		Sessions ↓	% New Sessions
		202 % of Total: 30.24% (668)	**54.95%** Site Avg 60.33% (-8.92%)
1. /category/3d/houdini/		71 (35.15%)	54.93%
2. /		70 (34.65%)	60.00%
3. /3d/houdini/maya-to-houdini-conversion-course-part-2a-particle-set-up/		18 (8.91%)	77.78%
4. /3d/houdini/maya-to-houdini-conversion-course-part-1a-where-commonly-used-items-in-maya-live-in-houdini/		5 (2.48%)	40.00%
5. /category/filmmaking/		4 (1.98%)	25.00%
6. /3d/naiad/naiad-rd/		3 (1.49%)	33.33%
7. /category/animation/		3 (1.49%)	0.00%

Fig 16.7 When you click on 'Direct', your primary dimension will be a landing page instead of a social source.

* Social – Obviously refers to the social network that brought people to your blog.

* Referral – This could be a link/backlink from someone else's site, either in their content or in the comments section in someone else's site.

* Organic search – How people found you through search engines.

B   I've highlighted this area for special attention as here you can directly measure the success of any campaigns that you've been running to bring people to your site. You can measure the value of visits through these campaigns versus the value of remainder visits (i.e. those that didn't come through this campaign). This will help you to keep your marketing focus on the most effective acquisition channels.

In fact, defining campaigns correctly is so crucial to the acquisition process that it deserves a chapter to itself. So now we are going to learn how you can really measure your campaign's success. This will go beyond just how many visitors a campaign brought you, but will show you how to derive value from those visits that we directly generate.

Chapter 17:

How to set up UTM tagging and create segments to really measure the success of your campaigns.

So how do you measure the success of your campaigns?

Before we can answer that, let's figure out what a campaign actually is and how we can define it. The best way for me to show you is via an example.

Earlier on in the year I launched a Maya to Houdini conversion course on my film and animation website http://www.digitopiafilm.com/category/3d/houdini/ (Maya and Houdini being two popular 3D software packages).

The way in which the campaign is going to bring people back to my website is via a link, e.g. if I want to bring people back to the first video in my series I'd set the link at the bottom of the social media post as http://www.digitopiafilm.com/3d/houdini/maya-to-houdini-conversion-course-part-1a-where-commonly-used-items-in-maya-live-in-houdini.

When I launched this course I ran two major campaigns:

- on Twitter
- on LinkedIn

Now the first thing I wanted to know was how well these two campaigns performed. How many people did Twitter bring to my blog compared to LinkedIn and how did those two groups of people behave differently?

To establish this for your blog, we need to define the campaign's source as either 'Twitter' or 'LinkedIn':

- Source = Twitter
- Source = LinkedIn

In each of these networks we can post in a variety of ways. On Twitter, it's possible to send a tweet just as plain text or include an image – in my case I chose to use image-only tweets. On LinkedIn, I could post the link as either a 'status update' or as part of a wider 'group post'.

The next thing to do is therefore to define some mediums relevant to each social network:

- Source = Twitter
  - * Medium = image
- Source = LinkedIn
  - * Medium = group post

The way in which we target our audience on Twitter and on LinkedIn is also of crucial importance. As you may know, on Twitter you can use hashtags to hone in on an audience, e.g. here I could use the hashtags '#animation', '#VFX' and '#CG'. On LinkedIn, I could post in one of the many groups, e.g. the 'Houdini group', the 'CG Society group' and so on.

So now I can define my campaigns in terms of source and campaign terms:

- Source = Twitter
  - * Medium = image
    - Campaign: hashtag = #animation
    - Campaign: hashtag = #VFX
    - Campaign: hashtag = #CG
- Source = LinkedIn
  - * Medium = group post
    - Campaign: group = Houdini Group

- Campaign: group = CG Society

So this is how we define the campaign. The next question is how do we now convert this campaign concept into a clickable link to put on the social network?

Building a custom URL

We are going to convert our link from http://www.digitopiafilm.com/3d/houdini/maya-to-houdini-conversion-course-part-1a-where-commonly-used-items-in-maya-live-in-houdini into one where we build in all the campaign variables that we've defined above. The way in which we do this is to add tags to the end of the link that define all the campaign parameters.

The tags we are going to add in are called utm tags and they contain our variable names. These utm tags are going to be placed at the end of our link. There's a host of online tools that make it very simple to come up with these utm tags. I use the URL builder native to Google, which you can find here:

https://support.google.com/analytics/answer/1033867?hl=en-GB

This gives you fields in which to enter your campaign parameters.

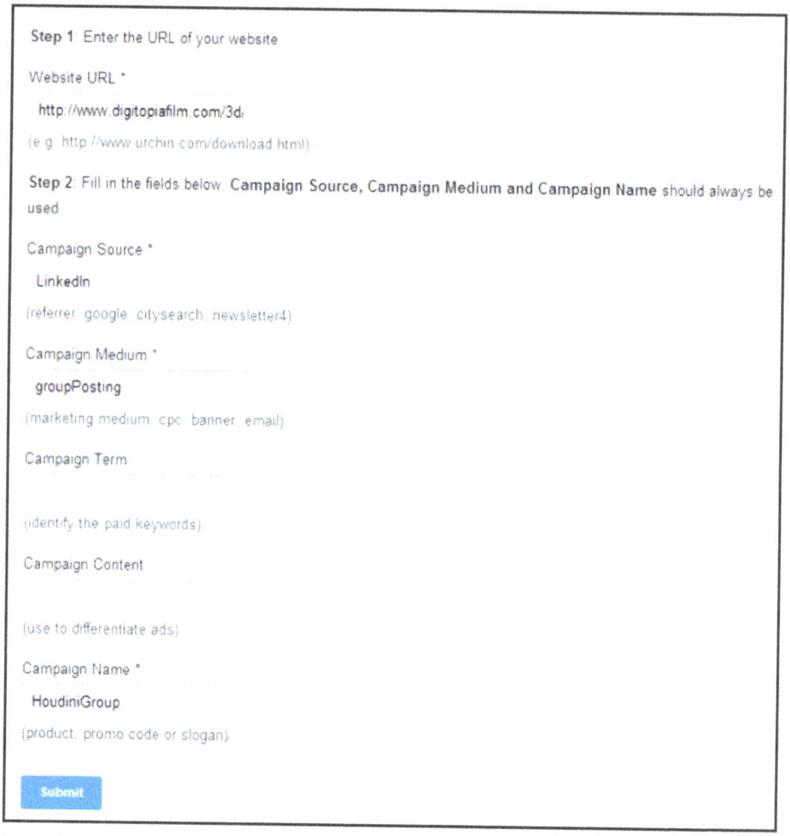

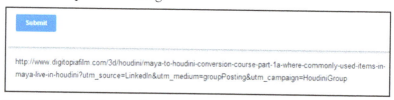

Step 1: Enter the URL of your website

Website URL *

http://www.digitopiafilm.com/3d/

(e.g. http://www.urchin.com/download.html)

Step 2: Fill in the fields below. Campaign Source, Campaign Medium and Campaign Name should always be used.

Campaign Source *

LinkedIn

(referrer: google, citysearch, newsletter4)

Campaign Medium *

groupPosting

(marketing medium: cpc, banner, email)

Campaign Term

(identify the paid keywords)

Campaign Content

(use to differentiate ads)

Campaign Name *

HoudiniGroup

(product, promo code or slogan)

Submit

Fig 17.1 Enter campaign terms into the URL builder. The fields marked with an asterisk (*) are required, and for more complex campaigns you can use all five fields.

When you've entered in the terms for your campaign, hitting 'Submit' will generate a custom URL which you can use on your various social networks or paid advertising.

Submit

http://www.digitopiafilm.com/3d/houdini/maya-to-houdini-conversion-course-part-1a-where-commonly-used-items-in-maya-live-in-houdini?utm_source=LinkedIn&utm_medium=groupPosting&utm_campaign=HoudiniGroup

Fig 17.2 Hitting 'Submit' will generate a link with all the campaign terms that you've specified.

You can see now the link that generated has all the parameters that we've defined.

Fig 17.3 here you can see the utm paramaters appended to the end of the url. Anything that comes after the '?' won't affect what the page loads.What happens next is that this visit is tracked as one that:

- Came from 'LinkedIn'
- Was of type 'groupPosting'
- Was posted in the 'HoudiniGroup'

You'll go through and make different campaigns in exactly the same way as this one. Now whenever anyone arrives at your site through these links, you will know through your analytics exactly which campaign brought them to you and how well your campaigns performed relative to each other.

One side note: On Twitter you may want to put this tagged link through a URL shortening service such as bit.ly, tiny.url or goo.gl. The URL shortener will maintain all of these tags so that you won't lose any information.

Analysing the performance of your campaigns

In Google Analytics, we can find these campaigns' details under the 'Acquisition | Campaign' menu option:

Fig 17.4 Where to find the campaign data.

Like many of the other views, this will bring up a graph and a table where you can see your dimensions and metrics. However, what is most useful here is that you can now filter any of the campaign terms to compare directly both the success of each campaign and how audiences from different platforms (various social networks, guest blog posts, PPC advertising etc.) actually behave once they are on your site.

Campaign	Acquisition			Behavior		
	Sessions ↓	% New Sessions	New Users	Bounce Rate	Pages / Session	Avg. Session Duration
	217 % of Total 29.56% (734)	53.92% Site Avg 55.58% (-2.44%)	**117** % of Total 25.88% (452)	64.52% Site Avg 59.40% (8.61%)	2.88 Site Avg 3.76 (-23.76%)	00:05:22 Site Avg 00:05:39 (-5.02%)
1 animationFilmJobs	**59** (27.19%)	64.41%	38 (32.48%)	72.88%	1.69	00:02:29
2 animationHashTag	**46** (21.20%)	65.22%	30 (25.64%)	69.57%	5.00	00:12:14
3 animation	**29** (13.36%)	41.38%	12 (10.26%)	58.62%	1.97	00:01:21
4 houdiniHashTag	**20** (9.22%)	25.00%	5 (4.27%)	30.00%	6.40	00:15:43
5 filmmakingHashTag	**19** (8.76%)	26.32%	5 (4.27%)	84.21%	1.47	00:01:08

Fig 17.5 The primary dimensions are based on your campaign variables (showing only the top five results for reasons of space). Here you can directly compare the results for all your campaigns.

From this figure, you can see which campaigns have brought in the most users and how those users have behaved. I can see instantly on Twitter that '#animation' is twice as popular with my followers than '#houdini' and '#filmmaking'. I can see that though '#houdini' didn't generate as many sessions, it did have the highest engagement with 'Pages/session' being a staggering 6.40 and the lowest bounce rate – here I really found an engaged audience.

The campaign 'animationFilmJobs' and 'animation' are LinkedIn campaigns that I ran, but although they brought me in a lot of traffic and new sessions, I can see that these sessions are not nearly as engaged as the '#houdini' and '#animation' traffic I acquired through Twitter (by looking at the fifth column 'Pages/Session').

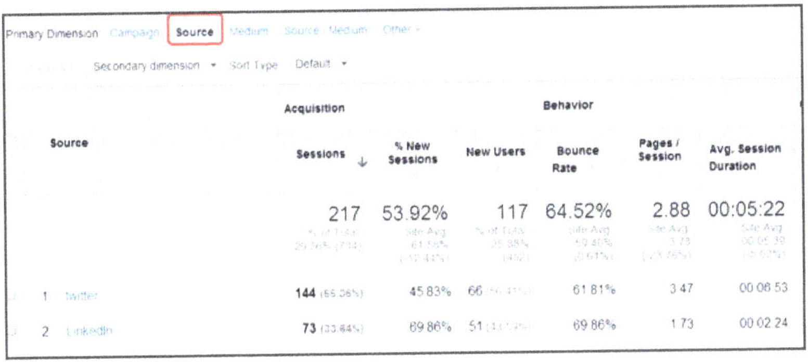

Source	Acquisition			Behavior		
	Sessions ↓	% New Sessions	New Users	Bounce Rate	Pages / Session	Avg. Session Duration
	217	53.92%	117	64.52%	2.88	00:05:22
1 Twitter	144 (66.36%)	45.83%	66	61.81%	3.47	00:06:53
2 LinkedIn	73 (33.64%)	89.86%	51	69.86%	1.73	00:02:24

Fig 17.6 'Source' will show the various platforms on which you are running your campaigns.

Fig 17.7 The 'Medium' link will display the various medium's performances relative to each other.

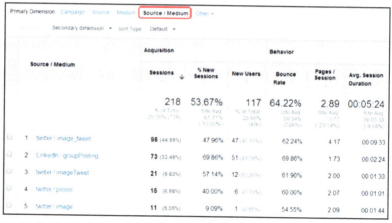

Fig 17.8 If you ran the same medium (think creative) on different platforms, you could compare the relative performance in the 'Source/Medium' table. In this particular case, I ran different creatives on LinkedIn and Twitter.

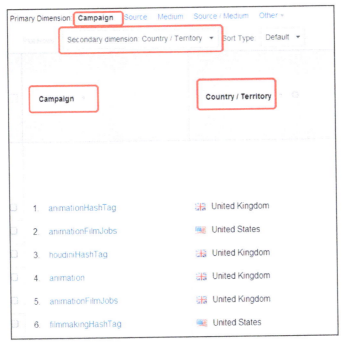

Fig 17.9 Of course you can combine any 'primary' and 'secondary' dimensions together to precisely understand every facet of your campaign.

Fig 17.10 The 'Other' option contains even further breakdowns for your 'primary' dimension – the most useful of these would be if you were running an AdWords campaign.

You can of course extend this concept and post the same image on Facebook, G+ and even paid-for advertising and compare the value you get from each platform. You could also run paid and organic campaigns across the same social media and then tag the medium as

'OrganicTweet' and 'PaidTweet' (rename to whichever network you use). This will help you ascertain:

- If the paid option is brining you value (think how much time and effort you would have to expend to gain the same results organically – that time and effort may be better spent writing your next blog posts).

- How much value you are receiving from each channel – by comparing your paid and organic traffic on the same platform, you will see whether you're overpaying for that traffic or getting a bargain.

When you do this across multiple platforms, you will quickly be able to ascertain where and how much to spend in advertising. Your analytics will help you cut through the marketing hype around each platform, as each social network will have a different audience demographic, and you will be able to assess whether that platform has the audience you are looking for.

Campaign analysis is one of the most powerful parts of the Google Analytics toolset. You can actually supercharge this data by creating segments out of these audiences and comparing how this particular audience behaves (and ultimately converts) versus other segments of your audience. In the next chapter I will show you exactly how to do this.

Chapter 18:

Segmenting users from campaigns.

I want to take a sideways step out of the 'Acquisition' menu set and talk about a global topic that you could and should use in any area of the platform – segmentation.

I'll keep the explanation of segmentation based on the acquisition model we are discussing and by the end of this chapter you'll know how to segment any criteria within Google Analytics.

Knowing the performance of your campaigns is very powerful, but you can take this a step further and supercharge your analytics by comparing the behaviour of those users you have worked so hard to acquire (whether that's through social networks, email distribution lists or paid campaigns) versus the traffic that you attract organically. This is how the concept of segmentation works.

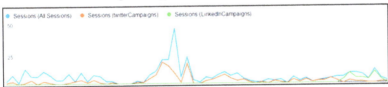

Fig 18.1 You can directly compare all your campaigns on the same timeline. The blue line shows the overall site performance, the orange line shows the traffic who came in on my Twitter campaign and the green line is the traffic that came in on my LinkedIn campaign.

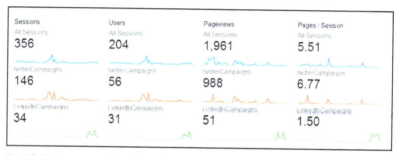

Fig 18.2 This view is from the audience overview section.You can compare directly how traffic from each campaign compares with any other traffic source from your website.

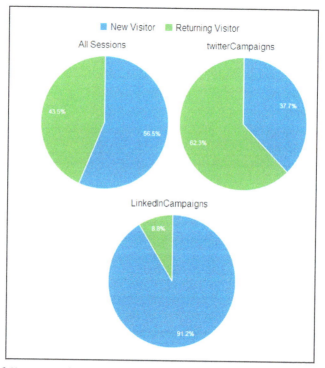

Fig 18.3 You can see the proportion of new visitors each platform is able to offer you and hence how much you can grow your user base in each segment.

Page	Pageviews	Unique ↓ Pageviews	Avg. Time on Page	Entrances	Bounce Rate
All Sessions	1,961 *% of Total: 100.00% (1,961)*	931 *% of Total: 100.00% (931)*	00:01:51 *Site Avg: 00:01:51 (0.00%)*	356 *% of Total: 100.00% (356)*	50.28% *Site Avg: 50.28% (0.00%)*
twitterCampaigns	988 *% of Total: 50.38% (1,961)*	466 *% of Total: 50.05% (931)*	00:02:02 *Site Avg: 00:01:51 (10.10%)*	146 *% of Total: 41.01% (356)*	52.74% *Site Avg: 50.28% (4.79%)*
LinkedInCampaigns	51 *% of Total: 2.60% (1,961)*	48 *% of Total: 5.16% (931)*	00:02:43 *Site Avg: 00:01:51 (47.33%)*	34 *% of Total: 9.55% (356)*	64.71% *Site Avg: 50.28% (29.70%)*

Fig 18.4 Segments can be listed in any view in all sections that make logical sense in Google Analytics.

Already you can see how powerful this concept of segmentation is in determining where to invest your time and money for the best returns. You can also see the reach of your social media presence and predict with reasonable accuracy how you could drive traffic back to your site based on any of your campaigns.

Let's go through the process of how you would set up a segment. I'm going to base the example on the campaign structure that we are currently discussing but I'll also show you how you can segment your traffic based on any criteria.

➔ At the top of any page you will see a horizontal strip where all your segments live. Click on the '+ Add Segment' link.

Fig 18.5 By choosing '+ Add Segment', you can create a new segment, use an existing segment or import one from a vast library of pre-built segments.

➔ Choose the '+ New Segment' button that has just appeared.

Fig 18.6 In this window you have the choice to add a new segment with the red highlighted button. The button next to this allows you to go through a library of segments, and I'd encourage you to have a look through this as there are so many useful pre-built segments which will save you a lot of time and add a huge amount of value and insight. Below the buttons is a table of the segments that currently exists. It's from here that you'd add any new segments into your view.

➔ Choose 'Traffic Sources.'

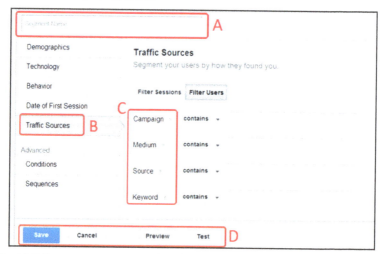

Fig 18.7 You can create a segment based on any five pre-defined types (left bar upper) or you can define your own (left bar lower).

Let's have a look at the constituent parts of this menu:

A   This is where you enter the name of the segment. Do take a moment to define a naming structure because this will be so valuable later on.

B   Here we're using 'Traffic Source' as we're discussing the topic of acquisition via campaigns. You can, of course, create a segment based on any other type – note that the corresponding options in step C will auto-update depending upon what you have chosen in this step.

C   Here you populate the fields with whichever of the variables you have defined in the previous step. In this particular case, we are using our campaign variables.

D   As well as saving and cancelling, you have the option to 'Preview' and 'Test' the segment before committing to either 'Save' or 'Cancel'.

Now you've created your segments, you can deploy them around your analytics and directly compare different acquisition methods. This will help you to quickly identify areas where you are particularly strong in acquiring traffic, areas that pull in high/low quality engagement traffic (understanding how traffic interacts with your blog) and where to focus attention to grow your user base.

Segmentation is strong in your sales pitch because once you identify which areas you excel at, you can use this data to prove your *reach* – that you are able to bring an audience to a particular page. You can also use this to predict how much engagement you could generate on your blog.

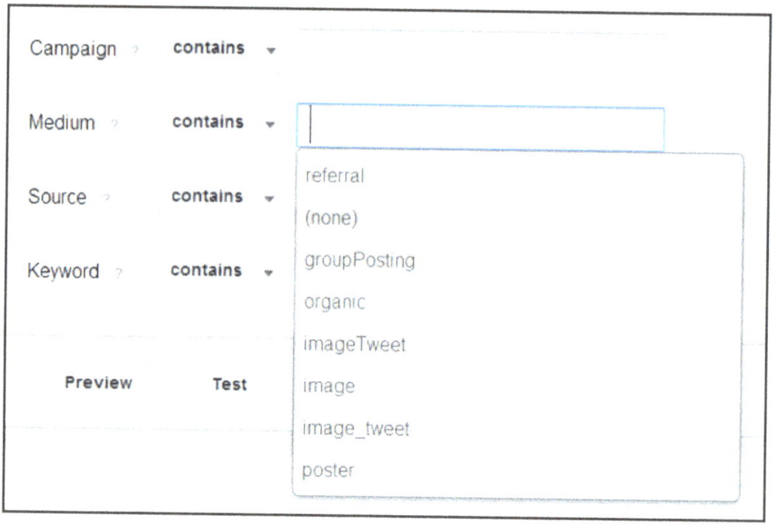

Fig 18.8 By clicking in any of the fields, a drop-down list of all the available options displays. This makes it super easy to create your segments.

Now that you understand why segmentation is one of the most important principles in analytics and how you are able to do it, a great place to start segmenting your audience is to base it upon any campaigns that you are running. Go and find out the real value and reach that you have in the various social networks, organic and paid search, and this will instantly tell you the best ways to bring traffic to your blog and which platform attracts the most valuable (highest engaged) traffic.

Chapter 19:

Acquisition – Keywords, AdWords, Social and Search Engine Optimisation.

The remaining sections of the 'Acquisition' area are to do with Keywords, AdWords, Social and Search Engine Optimisation (SEO).

Fig 19.1 The remaining parts of the 'Acquisition' menu set comprise 'Keywords', 'AdWords', 'Social' and 'Search Engine Optimization' (SEO).

The keywords and the SEO sections will tell you how well-optimised your blog is to generate traffic and how well your content meets the expectations of those arriving via searches. Whilst they are related, there is a key difference between the two.

Firstly, the keywords option is split into two sections:

Fig 19.2 You can analyse your keyword information based on 'Paid' and 'Organic' traffic.

These reports are similar to the others, but instead the primary dimension is based on the nature of the keywords visitors use to land on your site.

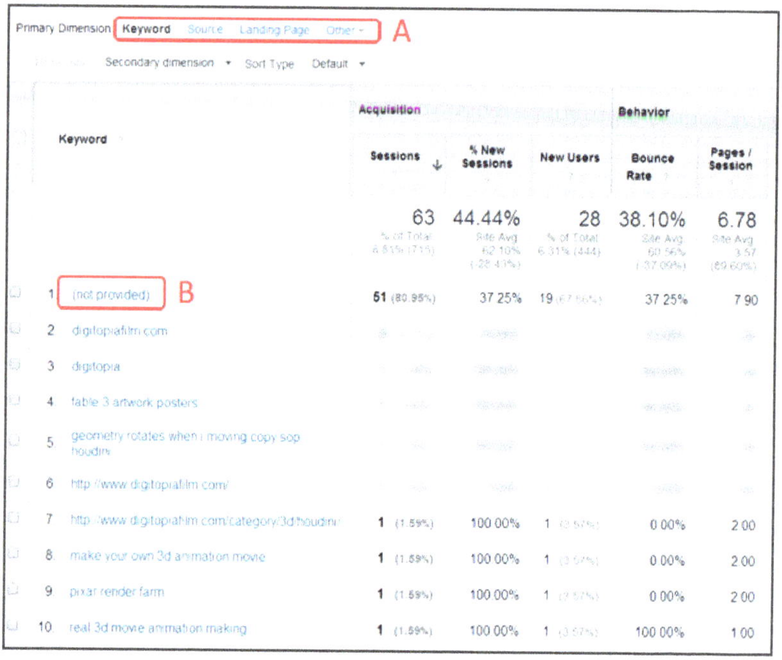

Fig 19.3 All the same measures and controls are available within the keyword table.

Two things to note about this table:

A   The primary dimensions are all based on keyword acquisition, i.e. 'Keyword', 'Source' and 'Landing Page'.

B   You'll notice the vast amount of keywords are 'not provided'. Not having these keywords available does somewhat hamper the usability of the report but there is still a wealth of information available in terms of traffic and engagement.

Before looking at 'Social', I'm going to jump straight into the 'Search Engine Optimization' section as it can be used in relationship with the keywords report.

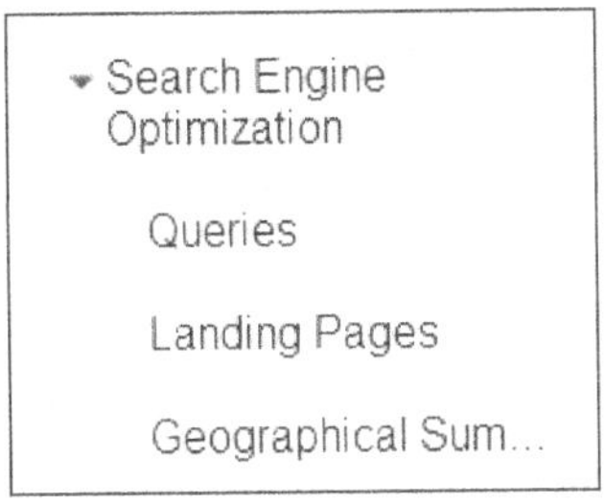

Fig 19.4 The 'Search Engine Optimization' menu is split in three parts: 'Queries', 'Landing Pages' and 'Geographical Summary'.

Linking Google Analytics with Google Webmaster Tools

Note that in order for this to display any data, you will need to enable Google Webmaster Tools. If you haven't yet done that, there will be a prompt on this page asking you to link the two accounts together. Essentially it involves:

- Signing up for a Google Webmaster Tools account (just sign in with the same Google login that you are using for your analytics).

- Fill in the form to give details of the website you wish to register.

- Google Webmaster Tools will give you back some code to paste into every page of your website. Don't worry, they don't actually expect you to go to every page – what they mean is to put it into your global template upon which every page is built (see Chapter 11 where we pasted in the Google Analytics code).

- Once the code is live, use the confirm link in Webmaster Tools.

- Google Webmaster Tools will go to your blog and verify that the code is there. Essentially this tells them that you do indeed have access and therefore own the site (i.e. you have admin rights to insert their tracking code into the template).

- Now back in Google Analytics, link Google Webmaster Tools to your Google Analytics account.

- There is a lag while this happens but within a few days you should start to see which search terms are bringing people to your blog.

The first part of the 'Search Engine Optimization' menu – 'Queries' – will give you a table of queries, the impressions and clicks they brought to your site, the average position your blog appeared in the query list and the CTR (Click Through Rate).

Primary Dimension: **Query** Other ⌄			
Secondary dimension ⌄		advanced ⊞ ⏀ ☰ ⇅ ⇞ ᛁᛁᛁ	
Query	**Impressions** ↓ **Clicks**	**Average Position** **CTR**	
	255 % of Total: 3.92% (6,500)	10 % of Total: 16.67% (60)	13 Site Avg: 250 (-94.05%)	3.92% Site Avg: 0.92% (324.84%)
1 sim reference	70 (27.45%)	0 (0.00%)	3.9	0.00%
2 houdini playblast	50 (19.61%)	5 (50.00%)	6.2	10.00%

Fig 19.5 The query table will by default only show visits from Google Property equal to 'Web'

Now there is actually a problem here with the way in which the data is presented, namely that if you went into your Google Webmaster Tools, the figures would not match. In fact, they wouldn't even come close. There are a lot of reasons for this. Google state that:

"Webmaster Tools data may differ from the data displayed in other tools, such as Google Analytics. Possible reasons for this include:

Webmaster Tools does some additional data processing—for example, to handle duplicate content and visits from robots—that may cause your stats to differ from stats listed in other sources. Some tools, such as Google Analytics, track traffic only from users who have enabled JavaScript in their browser.

Google Analytics tracks visits only to pages which include the correctly configured Analytics Javascript code. If pages on the site don't have the code, Analytics will not track visits to those pages. Visits to pages without the Analytics tracking code will, however, be tracked in Webmaster Tools if users reach them via search results or if Google crawls or otherwise discovers them.

Some tools define "keywords" differently. For example:

The Keywords page in Webmaster Tools displays the most significant words Google found on your site.

The Keywords tool in Google Adwords displays the total number of user queries for that keyword across the web.

Analytics uses the term "keywords" to describe both search engine queries and AdWords paid keywords.

The Webmaster Tools Search Queries page lists shows the total number of keyword search queries in which your page's listing was seen in search results, and this is a smaller number. Also, Webmaster Tools rounds search query data to one or two significant digits."

In my own research, I've also noticed that the only Google Property that Google Analytics shows is 'Web':

Fig 19.6 The only Google Property that Google Analytics seems to be able to display is 'Web', whereas in GoogleWebmaster Tools it defines 'All' as 'Image', 'Video', 'Mobile' and 'Web'.

In Google Webmaster Tools, you can find these 'somewhat' equivalent statistics in the left menu bar.

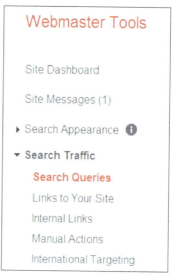

Fig 19.7 *Selecting your website on the homepage will give you access to this menu.*

At the top of the query page you'll see a 'Filters' button:

Fig 19.8 *In Google Webmaster Tools the filter is set to 'Web' by default.*

This by definition only shows you part of the results. You can change or clear the filter to see your results across all Google properties, i.e. 'Image', 'Video', 'Mobile' and 'Web'.

Fig 19.9 Clicking on the 'Filters' button will bring up the menu set, and clicking on the drop-down list under 'Search' brings up all the filters you could use.

Interestingly enough, when you go to the 'Landing Pages' menu in Google Analytics your results are fairly similar to the ones in Webmaster Tools (give or take the measurement differences that Google stated above). This is in no small way due to being able to see all the available properties appear under the 'Google Property' dimension.

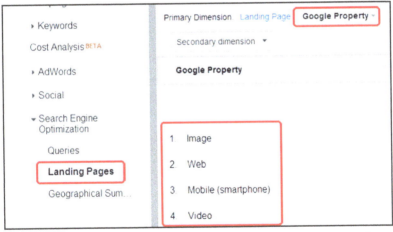

Fig 19.10 'Landing Pages' gives a closer approximation to the stats that you will see in the 'Top Pages' view in Google Webmaster Tools.

In the same way, 'Geographical Summary' gives closer results to the metrics in Webmaster Tools.

Establishing social significance

We've touched upon social regarding specific campaigns that you are pushing via social channels, but here 'Social' will tell you about traffic coming to your site via other social referrals, i.e. not just campaigns you've set up.

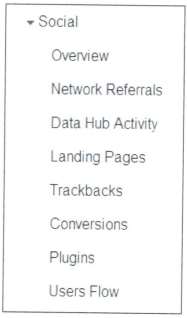

Fig 19.11 The Social Menu set, when expanded, will tell you about all traffic from social, i.e. how others are sharing your content and the traffic that is brought about from that social sharing.

▼ Social	Social Sources		Social Network		Sessions	% Sessions
Overview	Social Network	▸	1	Facebook	86	60.99%
Network Referrals			2	Twitter	33	23.40%
Data Hub Activity	Pages					
	Shared URL		3	Plus	19	13.48%
Landing Pages			4	t.news	1	0.71%
Trackbacks	Social Plugins					
	Social Source		5	WordPress	1	0.71%
Conversions			6	YouTube	1	0.71%
Plugins						
Users Flow						view full report

Fig 19.12 The 'Overview' will list the top level of social networks that have brought people to your site and shared pages on your 'Shared URL'.

Note here that if you click on one of the networks, it will automatically take you into the next menu option ('Network Referrals') but will filter it according to the social network that you've selected. In comparison, if you click directly on 'Social Referrals' on the left menu, the data you generate will be based on all the social networks, i.e. be unfiltered.

Social Network	Sessions ↓	Pageviews	Avg. Session Duration	Pages / Session
1. Facebook	86 (60.99%)	166 (60.58%)	00:02:09	1.93
2. Twitter	33 (23.40%)	74 (27.01%)	00:01:50	2.24
3. Plurk	19 (13.48%)	27 (9.85%)	00:01:04	1.42
4. Vimeo	1 (0.71%)	2 (0.73%)	00:00:33	2.00
5. WordPress	1 (0.71%)	4 (1.46%)	00:05:41	4.00
6. YouTube	1 (0.71%)	1 (0.36%)	00:00:00	1.00

Fig 19.13 The 'Network Referrals' table will show you the performance of the traffic from each social network. This is also a great way to segment your data (see previous chapter) to find out which networks are the most effective for your blog.

The 'Landing Pages' element is a really important table as it shows you which pages people landed on through a social network – that could be either a page that someone has previously shared or mentioned in a post.

Shared URL	Social Network	Sessions ↓	Pageviews	Avg. Session Duration	Data Hub Activities	Pages / Session
1. www.digitopiafilm.com/category/3d/houdini/	Facebook	67 (47.52%)	133 (48.54%)	00:01:57	0 (0.00%)	1.99
2. www.digitopiafilm.com/	Twitter	21 (14.89%)	49 (17.88%)	00:01:56	0 (0.00%)	2.33
3. www.digitopiafilm.com/category/3d/houdini/	Plurk	15 (10.64%)	18 (6.57%)	00:00:29	0 (0.00%)	1.20

Fig 19.14 This table becomes twice as powerful when you use the secondary dimension; the two secondary dimension types available are based on 'Social' (which houses 'Social Network' and 'Social Source Referral') and 'Time'-based, i.e. date, day of week, hour of day and so on.

So now you have a really good idea of how you can acquire visits to your blog and how you measure your marketing efforts. In the next section we'll look at how visitors to your blog engage with your actual content and how you can find out which of this content is the most valuable.

Chapter 20:

Understanding and measuring audience behaviour – does your content resonate with your audience?

The Behavior section is one of the most used parts of the analytics library, and in this section you will see precisely which are your best performing pages, who is seeing the different sections of your blog and how the audience flows through your blog. You can even create events to measure how often an action on your blog occurs.

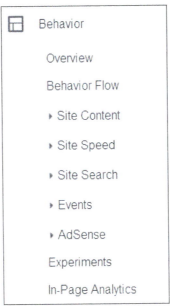

Fig 20.1 The 'Behavior' tab gives dimensions and metrics based on pageviews. This is where you can find out how your pages are actually performing.

Like in the other sections, you can start with an 'Overview' which provides a quick glance at your best-performing pages:

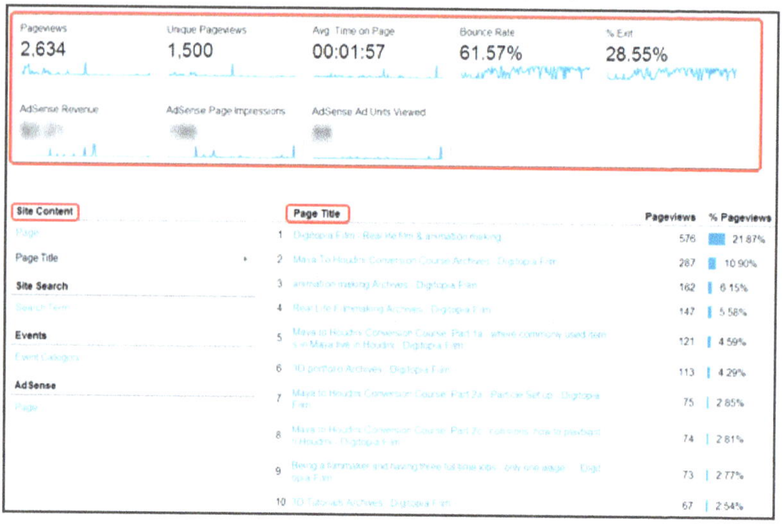

Fig 20.2 Top-level stats about your pages are displayed at the top of the page and below this you can filter the right-side metrics based on your selection from the left side. Here I have 'Page Title' selected on the left and therefore the metrics on the right are based on that selection.

The next menu is the 'Behavior Flow', in essence the same as 'Users Flow', which we covered in great detail in Chapter 15 (from Fig 15.30 all the way to the end of the chapter).

Fig 20.3 'Behavior Flow' is based on dimensions related to the page itself (A).

Expanding the filtering criteria in A will show you how the search criteria is based on dimensions that fall under the 'Behavior' category.

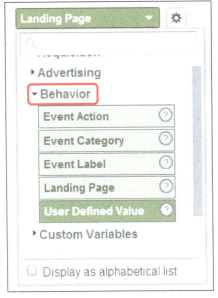

Fig 20.4 Google has done the work for you here and selected the filtering based on 'Behavior' dimensions — scroll up and down and you'll see that in all other aspects it is the same as the drop-down in 'User Flow' under the 'Audience' section.

Finding the most popular parts of your blog

The 'Site Content' section is where we'll find the most valuable information about our content and see how actual pages have performed:

Fig 20.5 The metrics for our site content.

Let's step through these one at a time.

As you might expect, 'All Pages' deals with all the pages on your blog. This essentially returns to you an uncategorised list of all the pages.

Page		Pageviews	Unique ↓ Pageviews	Avg. Time on Page	Entrances	Bounce Rate	% Exit
		2,634 % of Total 100.00% (2,634)	1,500 % of Total 100.00% (1,500)	00:01:57 Site Avg 00:01:57 (0.00%)	752 % of Total 100.00% (752)	61.57% Site Avg 61.57% (0.00%)	28.55% Site Avg 28.55% (0.00%)
1	/	561 (21.30%)	227 (15.13%)	00:01:55	200 (26.60%)	49.00%	24.42%
2	/category/3d/houdini/	287 (10.90%)	211 (14.07%)	00:02:14	163 (21.68%)	63.80%	48.78%
3	/category/animation/	162 (6.15%)	51 (3.40%)	00:01:14	5 (0.66%)	20.00%	7.41%
4	/category/filmmaking/	147 (5.58%)	57 (3.80%)	00:01:07	12 (1.60%)	58.33%	13.61%
5	/3d/houdini-maya-to-houdini-conversion-course-part-1a-where-commonly-used-items-in-maya-irive-in-houdini/	116 (4.40%)	107 (7.13%)	00:03:24	82 (10.90%)	70.73%	66.38%
6	/category/3d-showreel/	113 (4.29%)	32 (2.13%)	00:01:25	1 (0.13%)	0.00%	4.42%
7	/3d/houdini-maya-to-houdini-conversion-course-part-2a-particle-set-up/	75 (2.85%)	70 (4.67%)	00:01:51	51 (6.78%)	76.47%	66.67%
8	/3d/houdini-maya-to-houdini-conversion-course-part-2b-collisions-playblast-houdini-2/	74 (2.81%)	49 (3.27%)	00:01:58	15 (1.99%)	73.33%	33.78%

Fig 20.6 Notice how all the dimensions and metrics are now based on the page itself. You can add user and acquisition metrics by using the secondary dimensions box but the table will be pivoted on the 'Page' dimension.

From your table you will be able to see individual blog posts (which will have their full name defined) separate from the index pages of any particular section. In the figure above, the first four entries are category index pages, i.e. pages that hold a list of the posts in that category. '/' is the overall homepage and entries 2, 3 and 4 are the index pages of a particular section.

Fig 20.7 Each section of your site will have its own index page, defined as 'blogName / SectionName /'. This is the page on your blog that lists the individual posts within that section.

You can also order your data based on the categories themselves by using the 'Content Drilldown' option. This will split your results up in terms of the sections you have, and you can then drill down further into each of those sections.

Page path level 1	Pageviews	Unique Pageviews	Avg. Time on Page	Bounce Rate	% Exit
	2,634 % of Total: 100.00% (2,634)	**1,500** % of Total: 100.00% (1,500)	**00:01:57** Site Avg: 00:01:57 (0.00%)	**61.57%** Site Avg: 61.57% (0.00%)	**28.55%** Site Avg: 28.55% (0.00%)
1. /category/	**991** (37.62%)	489 (32.60%)	00:01:21	59.90%	21.90%
2. /.../	**561** (21.30%)	227 (15.13%)	00:01:55	49.00%	24.42%
3. /3d/	**397** (16.07%)	315 (21.00%)	00:02:24	72.62%	47.61%
4. /animation/	**211** (8.01%)	163 (10.61%)	00:02:54	75.00%	33.65%
5. /filmmaking/	**112** (4.25%)	55 (3.67%)	00:01:04	64.71%	19.64%

Fig 20.8 The 'Content Drilldown' table orders via 'Page path level 1', which essentially refers to the first subfolder in your URL structure. This tells you how the different sections on your blog perform relative to each other. Click on any of these to go in and see how the posts in that section performed.

A point of interest is that (in my case) the first item in the list '/category/' is actually the first folder for all my index pages. If you're running a WordPress site, each time someone clicks on one of your menu items or widgets which display a category name, the visitor will be taken to a page whose first folder is '/category/'.

Fig 20.9 Selecting any of the sections from the top of your blog (in WordPress) will take you to the category's index page.

For instance, if a user clicks on the 'Real Life Filmmaking' section on the top menu bar (or in any category-based widget), they will go to this page:

Fig 20.10 Notice the first subfolder is called '/category/'. This is what will show up in Analytics and essentially means that a visitor has clicked on a category title (either in the top menu bar or any associated widget).

To see which category your visitors have clicked on, click on the link '/category/' (Fig 20.8), which tells you how the index pages performed relative to one another.

Fig 20.11 Notice that when you click into any of the sections you are now taken to 'Page path level 2'.

WordPress users: When you do click on a blog post from any of your categories, your URL structure will revert back to what you expect it to, i.e. there'll be no intermediate '/category/' folder and you'll be right into the 'section/postTitle'.

The 'Landing Pages' and 'Exit Pages' give you corresponding metrics based on which pages people enter and leave.

How to create events

The next part of the 'Behavior' section that is of particular note is the 'Events' section.

Fig 20.12 The 'Events' section allows you to measure the events that you choose to define as significant on your blog.

Now it's quite likely (in fact, it's 100% certain) that when you go in here for the first time, you will see that all your events are zero, i.e. no events have happened on your blog.

Total Events	Unique Events	Event Value
0	0	0

Avg Value	Sessions with Event	Events / Session with Event
0.00	0	0.00

Top Events

		Event Category	Total Events	% Total Events
Event Category	›	There is no data for this view.		vie
Event Action				
Event Label				

Fig 20.13 You shouldn't be surprised that there are zero events on your blog, as you've yet to set any up!

Although this is the place in which you can see event reports, it's not where you set up your events in the first place. But before we go there, let's take a moment to actually figure out and define what an 'event' is.

An event is an action on your website that isn't measured by default in Google Analytics. This gives you the ability to track anything you can wrap an event tag around in your blog.

What does 'wrap an event tag around' mean?

It may sound a bit abstract but think about all the customised things that your blog does. You may have inserted video, you may be (and if you've read this far, you probably are) thinking of putting in banner advertisements on your pages, you may have PDFs, email opt-in forms and share buttons on your site. Each one of these doesn't have a specific section in Google Analytics, but Google Analytics gives you the flexibility to add them as events. Not only that, but you can assign them different names, categories and give each outcome a different value.

The way you do this is by adding an event tag into your blog's source code directly. It's really all very simple. Let's first look at the tag and then I'll show you where to insert it into your source code.

How an event tag is constructed

The way in which Google Analytics defines an event is to give it certain parameters. These are:

- Category*
- Action*
- Label
- Value
- Non-interaction status

Before we define these, it's important to know that only the first two (marked with an *) are required, whereas the other three are optional.

I'll define these by way of an example. Let's say that you have a set of social share buttons on your site and you want to know when someone shares your post via Twitter, Facebook or Google+ and give each of them a score. Through your segment analysis (see Chapter 18) you've found that visitors on Twitter read on average one page per session, visitors on Facebook read two pages per session and G+ visitors read three pages per session, so you'd like to allocate scores accordingly.

What you could do (although this would be the wrong way) would be to create three events – one for each social share link you create. These would then show up as three separate events in Google Analytics and you could compare and get all your conversions through the analysis as we've seen.

However, the correct way to do this is to define the whole lot as one single event with different actions. In this case, I'm going to try and keep things really simple and use only the 'category', 'action' and 'value' parameters to define the event:

- Social media share via Twitter worth one point
  - * Category: socialShare
  - * Action: twitterShare
  - * Value: 1
- Social media share via Facebook worth two points
  - * Category: socialShare
  - * Action: faceBookShare
  - * Value: 2
- Social media share via Google+ worth three points
  - * Category: socialShare
  - * Action: googlePlusShare
  - * Value: 3

You can see that all three events share the same 'category' name (because we've used the same 'socialShare' category). This means that when we go into Analytics, our event will be called 'socialShare' and will be distinct from other events, e.g. 'downloads', 'videoViews' and 'subscribeForms'.

Here are a couple more examples on how this can work. Let's say that you have four different places where people can subscribe to your email list:

a) a pop-up subscribe form

b) a form in the right-hand navigation bar

c) a form below the content

d) a form on a dedicated subscribe page

The event structure would now look like this:

- Subscribe list via pop-up window
  * Category: subscribe
  * Action: popUpWindow
- Subscribe list via right-hand navigation bar
  * Category: subscribe
  * Action: rightHandNavBar
- Subscribe list via form below the post
  * Category: subscribe
  * Action: belowPost
- Subscribe list via dedicated subscribe page
  * Category: subscribe
  * Action: dedicatedSubscribePage

The valuable data that you gain from this will help you lay out your blog better. You will know where to position your social media share buttons and your 'subscribe to newsletter' widgets, and can then extend this analogy to where you place your banner ads, affiliate links and the places where you sell your own products. You could even find out which audiences have different preferences and provide bespoke layouts accordingly.

So now you understand how events work and how you can structure them, let's look at the code that makes this happen.

The actual event code is written in the form:

_trackEvent(category, action, opt_label, opt_value, opt_noninteraction)

Yes, it looks intimidating but it's actually not really – all you have to do is substitute each of your own values where the parameters go. Remember that only the first two are actually needed; the others are all optional.

Going back to our examples, we can build these tags rather easily:

- Social media share via Twitter, worth one point
  * Category: socialShare
  * Action: twitterShare
  * Value: 1
    - _trackEvent('socialShare', 'twitterShare', 1)

- Social media share via Facebook, worth two points
  * Category: socialShare
  * Action: faceBookShare
  * Value: 2
    - _trackEvent('socialShare', 'facebookShare', 2)

- Social media share via Google+, worth three points
  * Category: socialShare
  * Action: googlePlusShare
  * Value: 3
    - _trackEvent('socialShare', 'googlePlusShare', 3)

As a quick aside, you'll notice that I've put in single quotation marks around the words but not the numbers. This is because you've defined the answer to the question of 'Category' and you've defined the answer to the question 'Action'. The words are known as strings. A string is essentially a text-based answer, like 'socialShare' or 'facebook-Share'. Any time you use a string-based answer like this, you must put it in single quotation marks to tell the code that this is a string-based answer.

The scores, however, aren't put inside quotation marks because you're picking from the list that Google provides, in this case a number.

If you choose the optional parameter of 'non-interaction', you have to select from an answer that Google gives (i.e. true or false), so you wouldn't put that between single quotation marks as you're choosing an answer Google defines for you.

All quite straightforward? Let's see the same for our email list subscribe forms:

- Subscribe list via pop-up window
  * Category: subscribe
  * Action: popUpWindow
    - _trackEvent('subscribe', 'popUpWindow')

- Subscribe list via right-hand navigation bar
  * Category: subscribe
  * Action: rightHandNavBar
    - _trackEvent('subscribe', 'rightHandNavBar')

- Subscribe list via form below the post
  * Category: subscribe
  * Action: belowPost
    - _trackEvent('subscribe', 'belowPost')

- Subscribe list via dedicated subscribe page

* Category: subscribe
* Action: dedicatedSubscribePage
  - _trackEvent('subscribe', 'dedicatedSubscribePage')

Deploying the event code

This code makes sense to Google Analytics, but it will make very little sense to your blogging platform. So the next step is to tell your blogging platform that this code is a Google Analytics code. You do this by 'wrapping' a Google Analytics 'wrapper' around this code. Yes, 'wrapping' and a 'wrapper' sound exactly like a 'wrapping' a chocolate/candy in a 'wrapper' and it is essentially telling your blogging software that this is a Google Analytics code and that it should ignore whatever is inside the wrapper and just send it back to Google Analytics as it is. Google Analytics will take it from there and unwrap the code.

The wrapper command for this is '_gaq.push([])'. Now you need to put the _trackEvent tags generated (in the previous step) into the square brackets of the _gaq.push command to look like this:

- _gaq.push([_trackEvent('socialShare', 'twitterShare', 1)])

Essentially we have wrapped our _trackEvent tags in a _gaq.push wrapper. Your blogging software will see the _gaq.push wrapper and know to ignore whatever is inside. This stops your blogging software from falling over trying to figure it all out and allows it to simply pass it back to Google Analytics.

One more thing you need to do is to tell your blogging software to *trigger* this code when an event actually happens, i.e. tell me it's a Twitter share when someone clicks on your '*tweet this*' link. You do this by using an onClick="" command, where you put the _gaq.push inside the double quotation marks. So your code now looks this this with the onClick command added:

- onClick="_gaq.push([_trackEvent('socialShare', 'twitterShare', 1)]);"

Note that there's a semicolon at the end of the onClick function just before the closing double quotation mark.

Now that it's set to trigger, you just need to place it alongside your actual buttons or links, wherever you've put the event. In the case of your 'tweet this' button, you'd nest this onClick action within the same area:

- <ahref="your twitter link" onClick="_gaq.push([_trackEvent('socialShare', 'twitterShare', 1)]);">Click here to Tweet this post</A>

As another example, let's say you offer a white paper download called 'analytics101' with a value of 5 that you want to create as an event. In this instance, your code would look like this:

- <ahref="/downloads/whitepapers/analytics101" onClick="_gaq.push([_trackEvent('whitePaper', 'download', 'analytics101' 5)]);">Download Analytics 101 here</A>

The optional noninteraction (opt_noninteraction) argument at the end of the event tag is where you set the event up to not record as a bounce, i.e. if the user was to land on a page, do the event that you wanted her to do, which meant she went to another site, setting opt_noninteraction to 'true', it would not record this as a bounce. In the above example of downloading a whitepaper from an external site, you would set the noninteraction to true to make sure that a single page visit didn't get counted as a bounce ="_gaq.push([_trackEvent('whitePaper', 'download', 'analytics101' 5, true)]);

This concludes what you need to know about Google Analytics. I've pretty much shown you everything from installing Analytics into your site, showing you around the main sections of your site and how you can define and find out Key Performance Indicators (KPIs).

You've also learnt numerous valuable techniques that will help you optimise your site and make it easy for visitors to complete the actions you want them to complete. You've learnt how to define which areas of the site bring the most value and where your audience comes from, both geographically and from the social media landscape.

In addition, you now know how to segment your audience according to any criteria and how to generate events on your blog. The only thing that remains is to put all of this into a dashboard which will auto-refresh and that you can use to demonstrate the value of your blog.

Chapter 21:

Creating dashboards.

By now you should have a strong grasp of how to find out anything that is happening on your blog using Google Analytics. I want to round this section off by showing you how to collate and present your findings to any potential partner(s). After all, it's not as if you are going talk them through each section of your analytics – you need to send them the salient points and the value proposition in a way that they can see and quickly understand.

Step forwards, the 'dashboard'.

Dashboards provide a superb way of pulling information together. With the ability to select almost any of the menu items we've looked at, dashboards provide an at-a-glance snapshot of how your site is performing and can be easily shared as a pdf file attached to an email. Sending a pdf file with the Google Analytics stamp on it always makes potential partners and advertisers sit up and take notice.

There are, however, a couple of limitations when you send a dashboard over, and during this chapter I'll make you aware of these and show you how to organise your dashboard for maximum effect.

First of all, at the top of any of the pages you will see an 'Add to Dashboard' link:

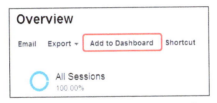

Fig 21.1 This link is available in almost every section, with the exception of the 'flow' reports (as those would be impractical to add into a dashboard).

This will open a dialogue box asking you to select a dashboard to add your report into:

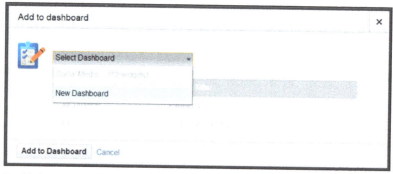

Fig 21.2 At the moment you likely don't have a dashboard to choose, so click the 'Select Dashboard' drop-down menu and choose 'New Dashboard'.

Now you can give your dashboard a name and choose which elements you want to add into it:

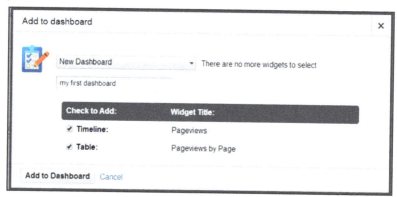

Fig 21.3 In this case I was in the 'Behavior' section, so got the 'Pageviews' and 'Pagviews by Page' metrics to add into the dashboard. You will get the appropriate metrics for whichever part you are in when selecting 'Add to Dashboard'.

By clicking the 'Add to Dashboard' button you will be taken directly to the dashboard you just created.

Fig 21.4 The first thing to note is that you are in the 'Dashboards' menu on the left.

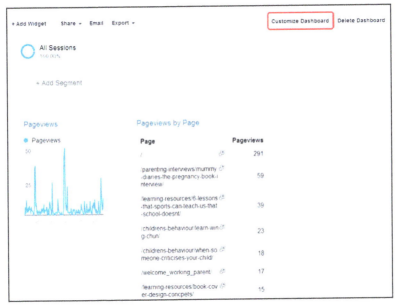

Fig 21.5 The default layout of the dashboard may not look so great when you start out. Use the 'Customize Dashboard' link at the top right to change the layout.

In this particular case it didn't work out so well because I included a timeline and 'by page' so ended up with very long names, which makes it hard to read when it's spread over two lines.

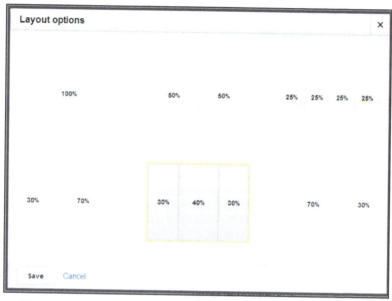

Fig 21.6 By default a three-column layout at 30%, 40% and 30% (highlighted in yellow) is selected — that's the reason why your dashboard looks quite cramped.

Play around with some of the other layouts to decide the best flow for your dashboard. It will largely depend upon the type of information you are trying to display. Consider using a 100% wide layout if you are including a timeline in order to give you plenty of horizontal space to best show off any trends in the data. If you're using pie charts, you may want to have each chart adjacent to the data that generated it, so a 50/50 layout will be very good for this. Get creative. It's very simple to change the layout again and reordering the widgets is as simple as dragging them into new positions.

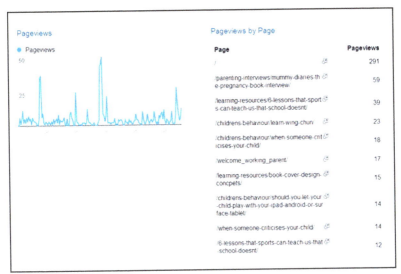

Fig 21.7 A 50/50 layout works reasonably well here and you can add more widgets (up to a maximum of 12) anywhere in the dashboard. Note that lists typically display the first ten results, so you can predict how far down the widgets will go and plan your layout better.

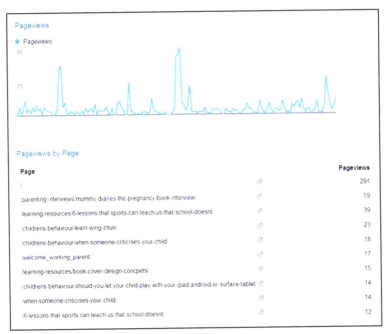

Fig 21.8 Compare the 50/50 layout with this one, which is a single column at 100% width. Which one is easier for the viewer to read?

Legibility should take precedence over style when designing these layouts. Again, you know your audience so you can make that call.

For the moment let's just stick with the two-column, 50/50 version as I want to show you how to add other widgets and change the layout.

Adding widgets to existing dashboards

To add more widgets into your dashboard, simply click the 'Add to Dashboard' button on any particular section you are interested in.

Fig 21.9 In any view that makes sense, you will see an 'Add to Dashboard' link at the top. In this example I went to 'Acquisition | Campaigns'.

Fig 21.10 Click on the 'Select Dashboard' to choose which dashboard you want to add your data into. To create a new dashboard, you have the choice of adding the 'Timeline' and the 'Table' (hidden behind the 'Select Dashboard' drop-down in this view).

After you've done this, you'll notice that the widget is placed at the top of your dashboard:

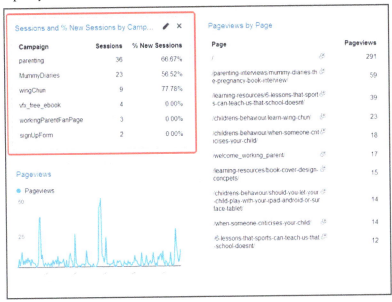

Fig 21.11 Any new widget gets placed by default at the top of the dashboard. To change this, simply drag it to the position you want.

When you have a lot of widgets in your dashboard, it can be cumbersome to start dragging them around and rearranging the layout, so it's useful to design your widget layout in reverse order, first choosing the items you want at the bottom of the page and then adding in the ones you want at the top.

You can create up to 20 dashboards, and each dashboard can contain up to 12 widgets.

To start customising your dashboards, hover over any of the widgets and click on the 'edit' icon in the top right corner:

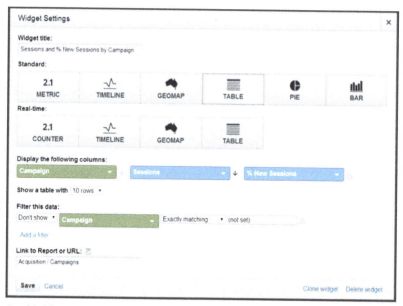

Campaign	Sessions	% New Sessions
parenting	36	66.67%
MummyDiaries	23	56.52%
wingChun	9	77.78%
vfx_free_ebook	4	0.00%
workingParentFanPage	3	0.00%
signUpForm	2	0.00%

Fig 21.12 The edit widget button will let you completely customise the display of the widget. The 'x' button next to it deletes the widget from the dashboard.

Fig 21.13 From the 'Settings' window you can change the title of the widget to something more meaningful to the reader. You can also change the display and any of dimensions and metrics, as well as filter the data.

The 'Clone widget' link at the bottom right is a quick way to edit a copy of the widget. Having a modified widget can help create context when placed beside the original. If you think of your dashboards as a way to tell a story, one widget should naturally lead the reader from one point to another, telling the story of your blog's value.

Comparing segments and date ranges in dashboards

I want to show you a couple more things that will supercharge your dashboards when pitching to a potential partner/investor. Firstly, each dashboard can have segments added.

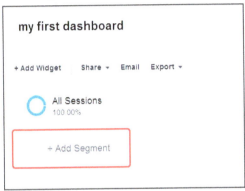

Fig 21.14 Adding a segment is a powerful feature that will help show the value of a particular stream that you are looking to sell.

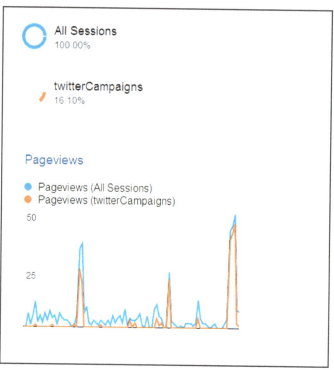

Fig 21.15 Comparing two segments side-by-side can tell your partner many things. In this case, I'm using this visualisation to demonstrate how I can use Twitter to drive traffic to my blog. You can use similar techniques to demonstrate your reach through any particular channel, e.g. any social media or even more powerfully a newsletter list you may have. This tells your potential partner that as well as having a significant social media following, that your audience is engaged and that you can use that engagement to drive traffic to any particular page / post.

When you add a segment into the data, it is shown side-by-side and you can add up to four segments into a view. This can work particularly well with graphs, although it can start to become difficult to view when reading tables.

◯ All Sessions 100.00%	✦ twitterCampaigns 16.10%
✦ Converters 22.03%	✦ Direct Traffic 16.10%

Fig 21.16 Adding multiple segments shows the effectiveness of your blog, far beyond showing pageviews and visitors. Here I'm demonstrating that I can bring people to my blog (the Twitter reach is in orange), that the pages on my blog are effective enough to get visitors to convert to whatever that page's goal is (in green) and that I have visitors who are now familiar with the URL of my blog (Direct Traffic in purple). So get creative and build a dashboard that demonstrates the value of your blog to potential partners.

The other thing I want to show you is that you can use the 'compare date' feature in the top right corner to demonstrate the growth of your blog, while still maintaining details of the most relevant periods.

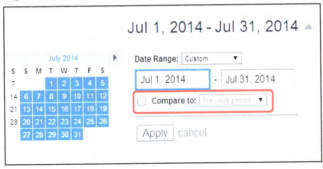

Fig 21.17 Using the 'Compare to' feature will let you compare any two time periods on the same graph. You could use the default 'Previous Period' which maps your current date range to the equivalent date range before it, e.g. if you have selected the current month, the 'compare to' will automatically pick the previous month. You can also choose to compare your traffic now to your traffic exactly one year ago, or any custom time period you choose (a second calendar will appear below your primary calendar to choose the comparison date range).

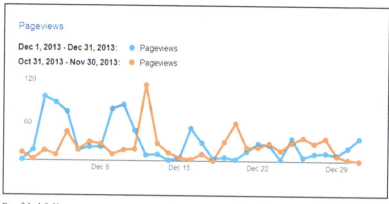

Fig 21.18 You can compare any two date ranges to show the growth in any of your blog's dimensions. This can quickly get messy when combining with segments, so if necessary create separate dashboards that tell a piece of the story. For example, you may want to show in one dashboard how your social media reach has grown over time and how that has converted, whereas in another dashboard you may want to present different aspects of your blog's growing influence.

Sharing the dashboard

The last thing to do is to package up your dashboard and send it to whomever you have identified. This is really simple to do.

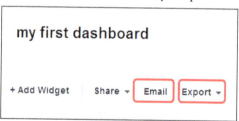

Fig 21.19 At the top of the page are the export options to 'Share', 'Email' or 'Export'.

Like many things in Google Analytics, the ability to share your dashboards is quick and simple. Choosing to 'Export' the dashboard will create a pdf version of your dashboard which you can then attach to an email. The 'Email' option even does this for you, creating an email directly from your associated Gmail account and giving you scheduling options to auto send the message.

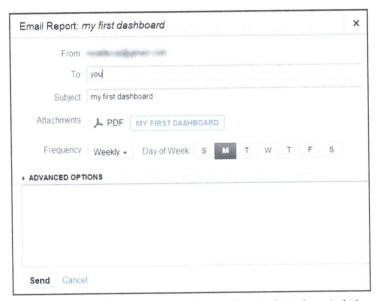

Fig 21.20 You can send the email directly from within Google Analytics (it links to your Gmail account) in the advanced options you set the frequency that the email should be sent at.

So now we've gone through all the main parts of Google Analytics. By now you should understand:

- how to install and set up Google Analytics on your blog
- how to link your Google Analytics account with your Webmaster Tools account
- what's going on in your blog
  * how many people are coming
  * how many are return visitors
  * where they are coming from
    - which countries
    - which sources
  * which devices people use to consume your blog
  * how people move around your blog
  * what the most popular pages and posts are
- how visitors are coming to your blog

- * which social sources they are coming from
- * how your SEO is performing and which are your valuable keywords
- how you can set up campaigns across different channels
- how you can measure the success of those campaigns
  - * how you can assess your reach across different channels
- how you can segment your audience into any criteria you choose
- how you can create and send dashboards

That brings us to the end of Part Four. In the preceding 21 chapters, I've given you everything you need to launch strategies to monetise your blog and you can measure the success of those directly now.

One of the first ways to do this while your plans take shape is to learn how to set up advertising on your page. In the next section, I'll show you how you can:

- set up advertising on your page
- place sponsors' ads in the most relevant sections of your site
- target those ads to the correct visitors

I'm going to cover ad servers and why these are important to you and I'll show you how to:

- quickly and easily install and integrate an ad server onto your site
- maximise your chances of gaining a click through to your advertiser
- set up any type of campaign that will allow you to laser focus your ads against the right content for the right visitor
- measure the success of your advertising campaigns
- report back to your advertisers the success of their campaigns
- find alternatives to AdSense and learn the right time to use one ad format over another and how to choose between them

For those of you who want to use AdSense, I'll cover this in great detail too.

Okay, I'll see you in the next chapter. The ride continues.

Part 5:

Ad serving – the complete guide to why you need it and how to do it right

Chapter 22:

Why do I need to set up an ad server? Isn't is easier to just paste the code onto my page?

I decided to title this chapter with the number one question people ask when they think about using a dedicated ad server. Setting up an ad server can scare many people and it scared me too when I first had to do it. It can seem daunting because of:

- the typically unfriendly front end

- the seemingly endless possible combinations of parameters you have to choose

- the multiple places where you seem to repeatedly enter the same data

- the fact that after you do it all nothing seems to have worked or something completely unexpected happened

- trying to decipher all the results and figure out whether that was a successful campaign or not

Yes, it is definitely a lot easier to simply put your advertiser's image into your blog and put a link back to their site, or even to paste some Google AdSense code into your page. After all, once you've done it, it's done.

But that's the whole point. Once you've put the 'image + link' or the code in, you can't do anything with it. It then becomes a static element and to change it would mean to change it across multiple pages. To put a new advertiser in would mean repeating the whole process across every page and post, and then having to redo the process across every new post that you write too. Even if you could do all this, how would you even know whether the campaign was successful or not?

The ad server may seem like even harder work to set up and implement at first, but after you've done that, you will have a robust, flexible and responsive system to manage all your advertisers and sell targeted ads to an audience that your advertisers want to reach.

As I've done in the rest of the book, I will walk you through every aspect so you can set up your ad serving platform quickly and easily and by the time you've finished reading this part of the book, you will fully understand how the whole process works and will be able to create any type of advertising campaign that will meet your client's needs. In the chapters on reporting, you'll be able to determine the success of previous campaigns and how to achieve similar results. I'll show you how to identify campaigns that are failing or not performing as well as you would like and how you can fix these issues. Finally, I'll show you how to automate the whole process so that you can set it up once and then get on with what you want to – blogging.

What is an ad server and what can it do for me?

An ad server is simply a server whose only job is to serve ads. In the simplest terms, you tell the ad server:

- which ads to serve
- how many ad impressions to serve
- when to serve them
- where to serve them to (in terms of geographically targeting your ad and also targeting your ad to a certain page/section)

The ad server in return will carry out your instructions and provide real-time feedback into the campaign's performance, telling you:

- how many ads have been served
- how many ads remain to be served

- when the ads were served

- where the ads were served (again both in terms of where geographically people clicked on your ads and on which pages the ads were clicked on)

To answer the original question in the title, yes, it probably is a lot easier to just paste some code into your site or throw in an image with a link from any advertiser into your blog, but as you can see, there would be no way to report back to your advertiser on how well their campaigns were doing. You yourself wouldn't know how well or badly any campaign was doing and therefore wouldn't be able to make any changes to the campaign's delivery. You would be forever rescheduling all the different creatives that are being sent your way and manually uploading them to every page of your blog. Don't gasp – people actually do this all the time. Luckily, you don't need to be one of them.

The whole process is actually a lot simpler than you think. Before I talk about the technical side of things, I will walk you through 'how' an ad server works. When you understand how it functions and the choices it has to make, you will very quickly figure out all the technical aspects of the setup (Chapter 24) and the way in which the ad server will execute its operations (Chapter 25).

Let's jump straight in.

Chapter 23:

How an ad server works.

The first thing to understand is that an ad server works on the simple concept of substitution. What that means is that you will place the ad server code on your site once – let's call this a placeholder – and from then on, the ad server will substitute whatever you ask it to into the placeholder.

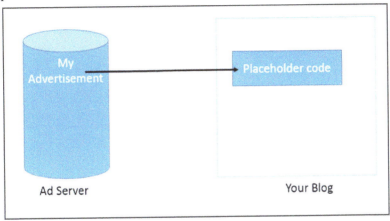

Fig 23.1 The ad server will replace the 'placeholder' code with whichever advertisement you tell it to.

You can choose whatever you want to put in there, for instance your client may ask you to display a banner ad and provide you with a link. In that case, you would direct the ad server to display the banner ad in the slot and point it to the link provided. You may on the other hand not have an advertiser yet, in which case you might want to drop in some adverts from an ad network/exchange, like Google AdSense (AdSense is Google's behavioural and contextual targeted advertising platform, which we will cover in Chapters 28 and 29). Alternatively you may have an affiliate account with any of the big retailers, in which case you would take your affiliate code and tell the ad server to run the affiliate campaign in any particular country a visit comes from or on any particular page of your blog. It all comes down to this concept of substituting any line item into a placeholder on your site.

The placeholder concept

Let's step through this a little slower. The placeholder concept seems straightforward enough – you place code from your ad server onto your site and the ad server then replaces its own code with the exact advertisement you specify. But as you know through your own web travels, advertisements come in many sizes. You will therefore need to create a specific placeholder for each size of advertisement. There are a dozen or so different ad sizes that you could use, but for the purposes of this book I am going to focus on the most popular ad sizes. If you want to change the ad sizes, simply substitute the pixel dimensions that I'm going to give to you with your own.

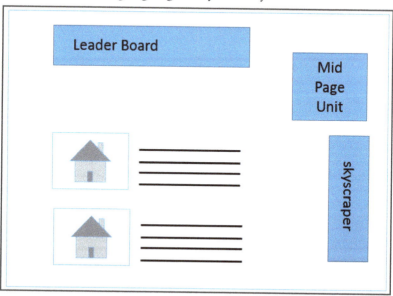

Fig 23.2 The most popular/best-performing ad units are the 'Leader Board', the 'Mid Page Unit (MPU)' and the 'Skyscraper'

The three ad units that we'll focus on are the:

- Leader Board 728px x 90px

- MPU (Mid Page Unit) which can either be 300px x 250px (medium rectangle) or 336px x 280px (large rectangle)

- Skyscraper 120px x 600px (regular) or 160px x 600px (wide)

You've seen these hundreds of times already but it's useful to know their sizes as you'll be plugging these into several places across your own blog, the ad server and any advertising partnerships you are about to begin (including in Google AdSense).

For each of these ad sizes you will be creating placeholders. You will generate placeholder code through the ad server and place the correct placeholder into your blog's template (see Chapter 11). It's important to put the correct placeholder code in the correct place in your blog, otherwise depending on which blogging platform you use, your ad will either be cropped or will expand and break your site layout.

You will also need to define on your site whereabouts you want certain sized ads. For instance, you will probably choose to have the Leader Board at the top of the page or the top of the post, an MPU and a Sky in the sidebar – this is a fairly conventional set-up and one you will have seen hundreds of times.

As we know, people can become myopic when it comes to the position of banner ads – 'banner ad blindness' refers to when people know where to expect to see the ads and automatically filter out those positions. Here's a tip: try having a Leader Board at the end of a post, just above the share buttons. This is because *people who read through the whole post are what we call 'engaged visitors'*. If you can serve a targeted ad to this person (and I will show you how to do this in Chapter 25) at the point where they are most engaged with your content, you can see how you have a better chance for them to engage (i.e. click) on the ad. Be creative, try different layouts and see what works for your particular audience.

Once you define which ads you want, you'll need to mirror those placeholders in your ad server:

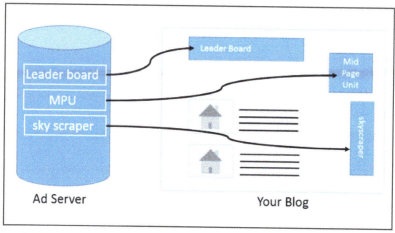

Fig 23.3 The ad server will generate code for you, which you then need to place within your blog's template (widgets in WordPress and Blogger). This is known as an ad slot, and the ad server will then choose the correct ad to place into the correct slot on your blog.

With this initial configuration set up, you are ready to define the various advertising campaigns within the ad server, which neatly brings us to the next concept.

The line item concept

When you define an advertising campaign, there are going to be a number of ways to classify each of them. Let's look at the example of a fictitious family optician who wants to advertise on your healthcare blog. From top to bottom you are going to want to:

- define the name of the advertiser
  * Owl's opticians
- define the name of the line item
  * Owl's opticians
    - *Owl's summer sunglasses*
    - *Owl's children range of glasses*

- define the creative that will be used in each line item
    * Owl's opticians
        - Owl's summer sunglasses
            - Owl's summer sunglasses – Leader Board
            - Owl's summer sunglasses – MPU 1
            - Owl's summer sunglasses – Skyscraper
        - Owl's children range of glasses
            - Owl's children range of glasses – Leader Board
            - Owl's children range of glasses – MPU 1
            - Owl's children range of glasses – Skyscraper

I've put the line item in italics in the above list. Some people will refer to these as 'campaigns', which in a sense is correct, but they may then refer to a 'back to school' campaign or a 'Christmas season' campaign and then send through new content for you to display during these seasonal times. By using the term 'line item', you can avoid such confusion. You can future-proof your ad serving operation by defining each of their 'campaigns' as individual 'line items'.

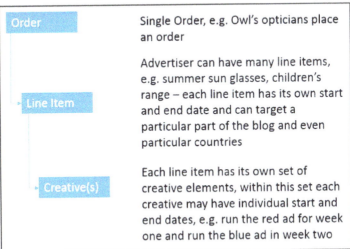

Order	Single Order, e.g. Owl's opticians place an order
Line Item	Advertiser can have many line items, e.g. summer sun glasses, children's range – each line item has its own start and end date and can target a particular part of the blog and even particular countries
Creative(s)	Each line item has its own set of creative elements, within this set each creative may have individual start and end dates, e.g. run the red ad for week one and run the blue ad in week two

Fig 23.4 Each line item belongs to an advertiser and each line item contains different creative(s).

In DoubleClick for Publishers (DFP, which is the ad server I'm going to walk you through), the order will just ask for basic information, such as:

- name of the order (e.g. Owl's Opticians)
- advertiser (this would be the same as the name of the order above)
- trafficker (e.g. you)
- labels (optional)

It's in the line item itself where you will load in most of the details about how the ad should be configured, including:

- what sizes the ads will be (e.g. Leader Boards, MPUs, Skyscrapers)
- start and end dates
- how many impressions to deliver
- how much they've paid for the ads
- how you want the ads to be delivered (e.g. evenly, frontloaded, as fast as possible)
- any type of targeting you want to apply (e.g. show them only in North America, show/exclude them on certain pages)

The creative section is where you will specify details that links directly to the creative(s):

- upload the creative (e.g. the artwork that has been sent to you)
- what the creative start and end times are (these can differ to the line items start and end times when you have more than one creative, e.g. display the red creative during week one and the blue creative during week two)
- where the creative should actually link to (e.g. point the leaderboard to mysite.com/page1 and the skyscraper to mysite.com/page2)

You've now learnt the anatomy of an ad, how a single order may have many line items, how a single line item may have many creative elements to it and what the controls at each level do.

In the next chapter, I'll step through each of these parameters and we'll look in detail on how you can adjust each of these and the effect they have on the delivery of the whole order.

Chapter 24:

Setting up and installing DoubleClick for Publishers (DFP) on your blog.

In the last two chapters, we've gone through how an ad functions and the architecture of how an ad server calls and decides which ad to show. In this chapter we'll go step by step to show you how to:

- set up the DFP environment
- create ad units
- install ad units on your blog

First of all, let's have a tour inside DFP and discover what the main areas are.

To begin with, you'll need to log into your DFP account. If you have a Google account (and if you've been following along up until this point you do), go to www.google.com/dfp and log in using the same login details as for Google Analytics.

DFP is laid out in much the same way as many of the Google products and in the top left you'll see the main areas:

Fig 24.1 Here you can navigate quickly between the orders, inventory, reports and admin sections.

On the right-hand top corner you have access to your search, person-alisation, messages and help settings.

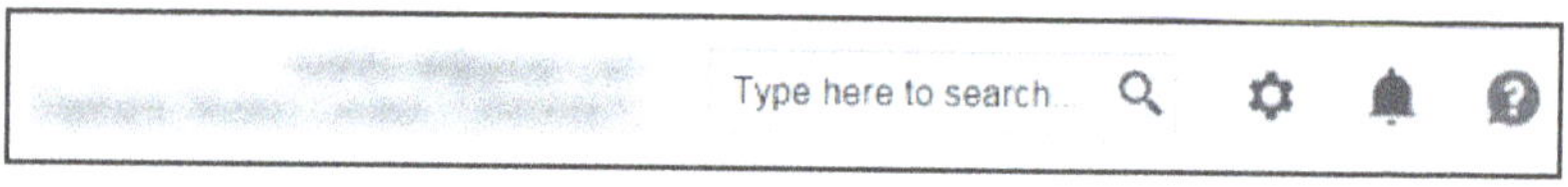

Fig 24.2 *On the top right are settings that relate to your account.*

Which area you are in (see Fig 24.1) will determine what you see on the left side menu. While in the 'Orders' area, you will see a menu list relating to the orders:

Fig 24.3 *The main sections in DFP were outlined in the previous chapter. Clicking on any of these will expand them for you to control any attribute you like.*

Set-up Part 1: The 'Admin' area

Starting with the top menu, the 'Admin' tab allows you to set up the details of your website and will generate a 'Network Code'. This basically associates the tags you generate with your account. There really isn't much in here that you need to worry about because when you sign in to activate your account this will all be set up for you. I just want to highlight two parts of the 'Admin' section that you could find useful going forwards. Those are how to create users and assign roles to different users that you may have working with/for you.

Fig 24.4 *'Users' will allow you to add new users into your system and 'Roles' allows you to set pre-defined roles to any users that you create.*

Setting up users is very simple – just hit the 'New user' button and fill out the corresponding form.

Fig 24.5 *Press the 'New user' button and fill out the simple form.*

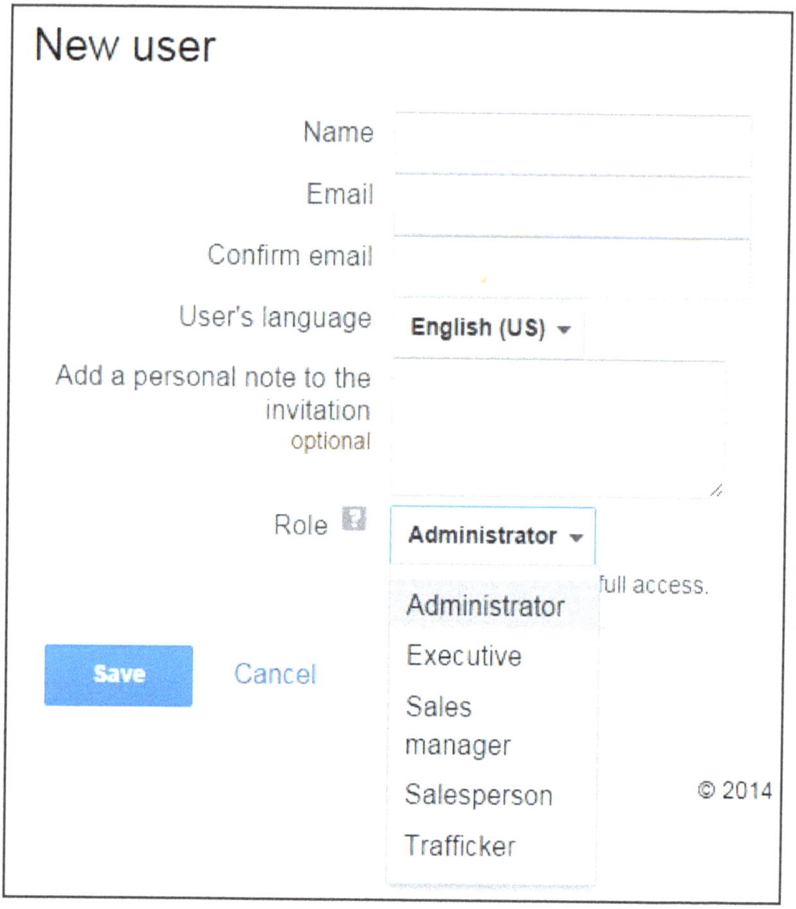

New user

Name	
Email	
Confirm email	
User's language	**English (US)** ▾
Add a personal note to the invitation optional	
Role 🔳	**Administrator** ▾

ull access.

Administrator

Executive

Sales manager

Salesperson

Trafficker

Save   Cancel

© 2014

Fig 24.6 In this form you will be able to select the 'Role' you want to apply to the user.

The option to change roles for a user is also available in the 'Roles' menu.

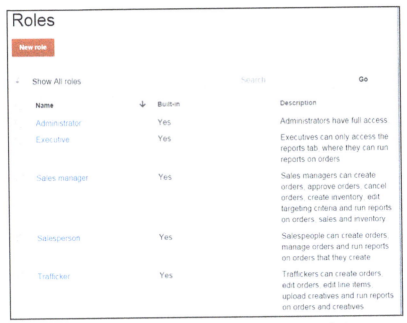

Roles

New role

Show All roles   Search   **Go**

Name	↓	Built-in	Description
Administrator		Yes	Administrators have full access
Executive		Yes	Executives can only access the reports tab, where they can run reports on orders
Sales manager		Yes	Sales managers can create orders, approve orders, cancel orders, create inventory, edit targeting criteria and run reports on orders, sales and inventory
Salesperson		Yes	Salespeople can create orders, manage orders and run reports on orders that they create
Trafficker		Yes	Traffickers can create orders, edit orders, edit line items, upload creatives and run reports on orders and creatives

Fig 24.7 In the 'Roles' menu you will see the definition of the types of roles you can apply to users and even create a new role too.

Set-up Part 2: The 'Inventory' area

The 'Inventory' area is where we are going to create our ad units. We are not going to define what goes into the ad units (that comes in the next chapter), but here we will:

- define our ad units' sizes

- generate tags from the different types and sizes of ad units

- copy and paste the code from DFP into our blogging platform

As we learnt in Chapter 23, there are lots of different sizes of banner ads that we can use. In this setup we'll stick to the sizes we defined earlier.

The first thing to do is to click on the 'Inventory' tab and select 'Ad units':

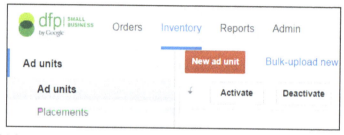

Fig 24.8 Press the large red 'New ad unit' button to create a new ad unit.

Fig 24.9 Add as many new ad units as you need for each size of ad.You'll need to create a new ad unit if you have specific ad units that you want to target to a certain part of your blog, e.g. a Leader Board on the homepage and a Leader Board on 'About Me' page would mean you'd need to create two Leader Board ad units.

Let's step through some of these settings.

1) Name – This sounds obvious, but do actually spend some time to come up with a naming structure that makes sense for your own blog. For example, I've used the following construct:

websiteName_websiteSection_adUnitSize

What this essentially means is that all my ad units follow the same naming convention. Because I run many sites, I use an abbreviated name (e.g. DF2) so that I can see all the ads on my DF2 site. I then have several sections, one of which is 3D Portfolio, so I call that 3dPortfolio and then as I run the Leader Board, MPU and Sky formats, I append that on the end.

Fig 24.10 I can then target different creative(s) to each section on my site. For example, I have sections on '3D' and 'writing' on my blog, I create distinct ad units for each section so that I can display the correct advertising in each section, i.e. '3D software' ads in the '3D' sections and 'writing courses' ads in the 'writing' sections.

2) The size is where you define the ad unit sizes you want. Just clicking in the box will display a drop-down list of the ad sizes available:

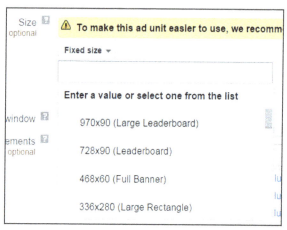

Fig 24.11 The full list of ad sizes is available by clicking in the box, which also has an auto-complete feature. Note that you'd only want to select one ad size in each ad unit except in the case of the MPU, where you could choose both the large (336 x 228) or the regular size (300 x 250) sized rectangle.

3) I'd recommend setting the target window to '_blank', which will open the corresponding ad in a new window/tab on the visitor's browser.

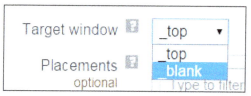

Fig 24.12 Leaving 'Target window' set to '_top' will open the ad over your current blog page.You probably don't want the visitor to leave your site, so set the 'Target window' to '_blank' to open the ad link in a new window or tab (depending upon the user's browser).

4) The optional 'Placements' box allows you to place ads on certain parts of your blog, e.g. in one of my examples I want to separate out 3D ads from writing ads, so I use placements here.

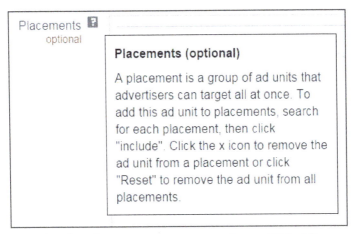

Fig 24.13 If you have distinct sections on your sites where you'd like different advertisers to advertise, then placements are a good way to accomplish this.

Once you are happy that you have created the various ad units, you will see them listed in the 'Ad Units' section (see Fig 24.10 for an example). When you're ready, hit the 'Generate tags' link, which will give you the code to copy and paste into your blogging platform.

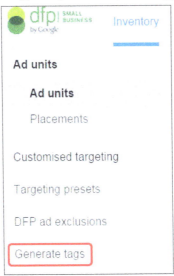

Fig 24.14 Hitting 'Generate tags' will give you the code to copy and paste back into your blog.

WARNING: *Every time you hit 'Generate tags', the system will generate new tags for your blog. What this means is that if you have already pasted tags previously into your blog and then add a new unit, hitting 'Generate tags' again will regenerate all your existing tags. All your old tags that you pains-takingly put into you blog will be lost. I found this out the hard way. Immedi-ately at the end of this section (Fig 24.26) I will show you how to generate new tags for new ad units without losing the existing tags.*

A window will appear with the code that you need to copy and paste. The code will come in two parts:

- the first part that you put into the template of the blog
- the second part that you put into the exact place where you want your ad to appear

So what does this mean in practice?

The first part is something that you place in your blog's template file, and I'll show you two examples – in WordPress and in Blogger – of this. The second part (where you place your exact ad units) will be done through the use of widgets (if you choose to have them in sidebars) or directly in code if you want the ad to appear in the body of an article. Let's start off with a WordPress setup.

WordPress implementation

In WordPress, go into the settings page where you insert header/footer scripts. In the header section, copy and paste the header script from DFP.

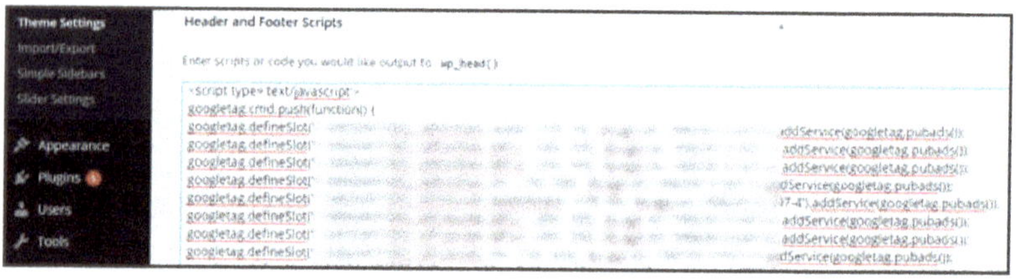

Fig 24.15 In the header section, paste the DFP script to define what these ad units will be called. Think of it as a reservation system, without which the placement of the

ads won't work (becauseWordPress won't know to be expecting the ad when you call it in a widget/code (see next part)).

Now that you've defined this, take each ad unit's DFP tag (I'll show you how to generate the placement tag in the next section) and put it into the individual widgets (if you want them in the sidebar, e.g. MPUs and Skyscrapers).

Fig 24.16 From the 'Appearance' menu set, select 'Widgets', drag across a 'Text' widget into your sidebar and place it where you would like your ad unit to appear.

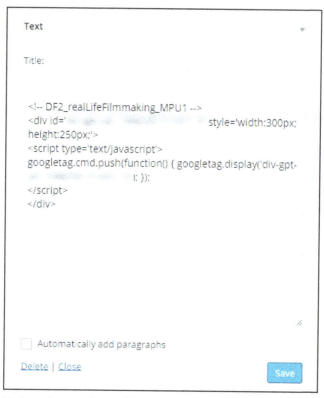

Fig 24.17 Paste the second part of the DFP tag (the bit that specifies that it should go in the body) into the text widget.

You can, of course, equally paste the generated tag directly into the blog post itself.

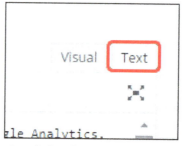

Fig 24.18 If you paste the code directly into the page/post, make sure you are in 'Text' mode in the edit page/post creation stage for the JavaScript to work.

Blogger implementation

In Blogger, the setup is almost identical. The header code needs to be placed in the edit HTML link:

Fig 24.19 On the left bar menu select the 'Template' link.

Fig 24.20 Choose the 'Edit HTML' button to get access to your source code for the file.

Fig 24.21 Anywhere between the <head> and </head> tags you can paste the DFP header code in, obviously being careful not to insert it in the middle of another procedure.

Fig 24.22 To insert the ad units into your pages' layout, first click 'layout' in the left menu.

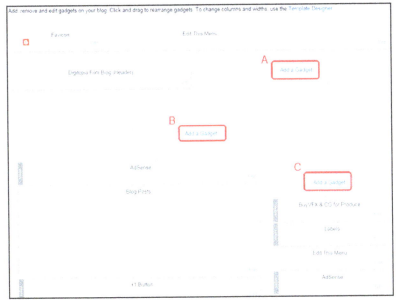

Fig 24.23 Hit the 'Add a Gadget' link to add the text gadget to your page.

Here you can add gadgets in three different areas:

A   Will add the gadget to the header.

B   Will add the gadget into the body of your post, dragging
         above the 'Blog Posts' gadget will put it above and if you
         want your ad below, you can drag it below the 'Blog Posts'
         rectangular box.

C   Will add the gadget to the right sidebar.

*Fig 24.24 Select the 'HTML/JavaScript' option to open up the window into which
you can paste your code.*

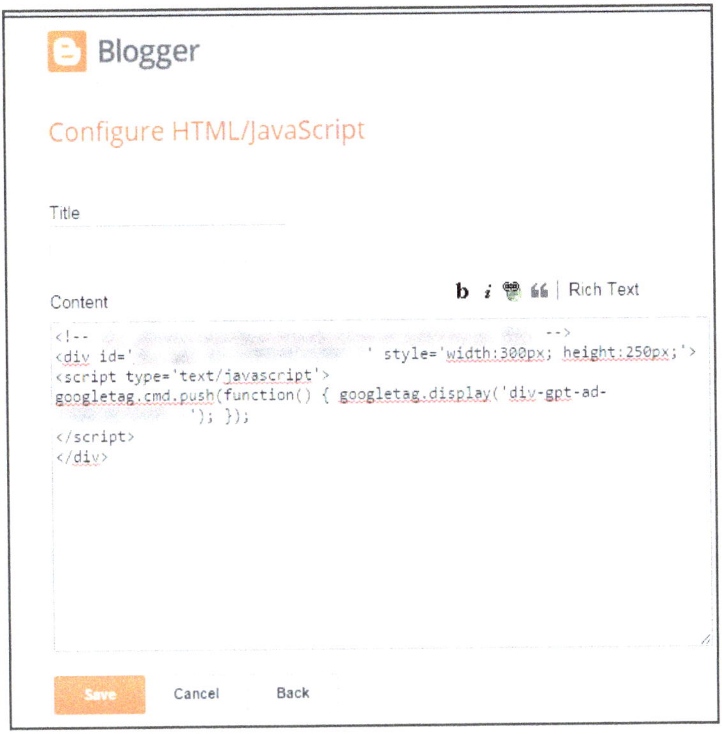

Configure HTML/JavaScript

Title

Content

b *i* 🌐 66 | Rich Text

```
<!--                                              -->
<div id='                    ' style='width:300px; height:250px;'>
<script type='text/javascript'>
googletag.cmd.push(function() { googletag.display('div-gpt-ad-
                   '); });
</script>
</div>
```

Save   Cancel   Back

Fig 24.25 Now paste the second part of the DFP code into this box and hit 'Save'. Don't worry about giving it a title, as the title may appear in the blog above the ad unit.You can then drag the widget to wherever you'd like it to appear in the blog.

I mentioned earlier in this section that when you create a new ad unit, there is a danger of overwriting you generated DFP ad tags. The way to avoid inadvertenly overwriting all your ad tags (which you have now pasted into your templates) is to go into the newly created ad unit and hit the 'Generate Tag' button in the top corner.

Fig 24.26 What this does is to generate a tag just for the new ad unit.

You need to paste just the line containing the new ad unit name into the global header line. The rest of the ad unit tag can be placed in the widget.

In this chapter you have learnt how to:

- configure DFP

- create ad units

- generate ad unit tags for your header and body (i.e. the tags to put in the widgets)

- install them onto your blog's header template file and into the widgets

In the next chapter we are going to start creating the adverts themselves and learn about all the settings around the ads. They will now start to appear on your blog.

Chapter 25:

How to create your ads in Double Click for Publishers (DFP).

In the previous two chapters we've gone through how an ad functions and the architecture of how an ad server calls and decides which ad to show. You've learnt how to configure DFP, how to install it on your blogging platform and how to create ad units. In this chapter, we'll go through how to create your first ad campaign. Let's divide this into the three areas we've looked at, namely:

- creating an order
- creating a line item
- adding a creative(s) to that line item

With this approach, you will learn where each setting is and logically why it is there. You will be able to understand why certain ads are appearing or not appearing and you will be able to tailor your advertising packages to your advertiser's needs.

Fig 25.1 Under the 'Orders' tab you will see the three main areas: 'Orders', 'Line Items' and 'Creatives'.

Interestingly enough, you will only need to go into the 'Orders' left-hand menu when you set an order. There's very little in the way of amendment you need to do here and you will be spending most of your time in the other two areas, 'Line Items' and 'Creatives', adjusting order delivery and uploading new creative copy that you've been sent.

First of all let's look in 'Orders'.

Fig 25.2 The 'Orders' menu will show you all the different states your orders are currently categorised under.

Creating a new order

Whichever view you are in, you will have the opportunity to create a 'New Order'.

Fig 25.3 The 'New order' button will allow you to enter top-level details about your advertiser.

From here you'll be taken to a page where you can enter details for both the order and the line item.

Fig 25.4 You can see exactly how basic the 'New order' fields are – they are basically just a way to categorise your line items so that they fall under the right advertiser. Note that the 'Trafficker' will match the DFP login the order is created under, i.e. it will be your own login. If you've created another user then it will be their name if they were to log in.

Directly below this box is the place where you enter the line item details. This is broken down into four sections:

- defining the line items
- setting up its main parameters
- adjusting its delivery
- targeting it to parts of your blog or to certain geographies

Creating a line item

Once the order has been created it's time to populate that order with a line item / several line items.

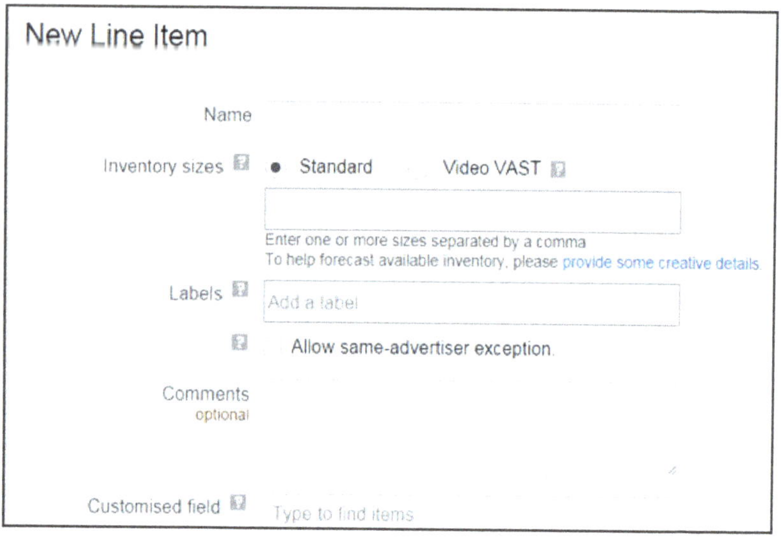

New Line Item

Name

Inventory sizes • Standard   Video VAST

Enter one or more sizes separated by a comma
To help forecast available inventory, please provide some creative details

Labels   Add a label

Allow same-advertiser exception.

Comments
optional

Customised field   Type to find items

Fig 25.5 The 'New Line Item' settings allow you to define the ad unit sizes. You can have more than one ad unit size in the line item.

Amongst the obvious things here like 'Name' and 'Comments', the most important field to determine is the type of line item you create, i.e. the 'Inventory sizes' field. This is determined by what you have sold to your advertiser. If you have sold a Leader Board then you will only enter in a Leader Board here; if you have sold a Leader Board, a Skyscraper and a MPU, then you will define all three. You'll actually upload the different creative(s) in the third part of the process. For now, think of this is as basically holding those ad unit spots for you.

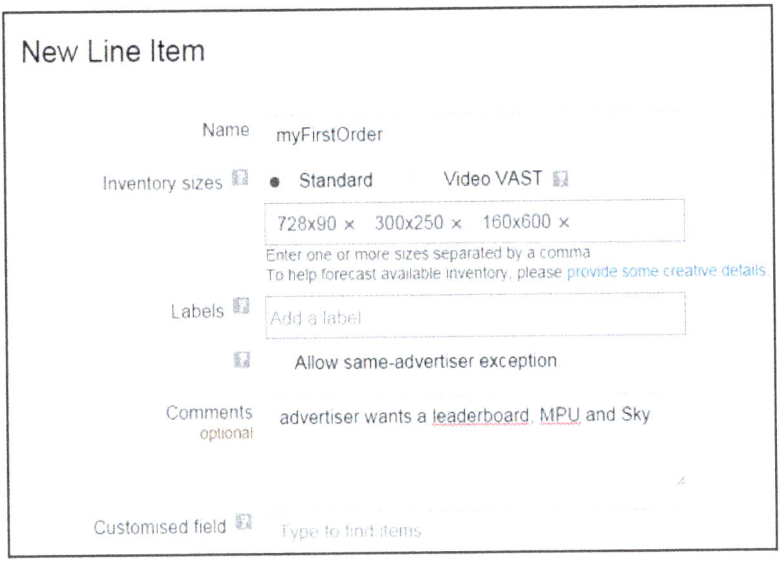

Fig 25.6 In this example I am holding a Leader Board, MPU and a Skyscraper in the 'Inventory sizes' field.

Setting line item priority

Fig 25.7 In the 'Settings' part you set the 'flight details', entering the start and end dates and the amount of 'Impressions' or 'Clicks' you are selling.

There are many options for the 'Type' setting, each of which has its own definition:

Delivery priority

Sponsorship: Highest-ranking line item type for fixed-position and time based campaigns.

Standard: For impression-based campaigns.

Network, bulk and price priority: For unsold inventory.

House: Lowest-ranking line item type. Typically used for ads that promote products and services chosen by you.

Fig 25.8 The different delivery types set the priority on how this line item may be delivered ahead of other competing line items.

Stepping through each type

- Sponsorship: These will deliver first, ahead of any other line item. You can't set a quantity on sponsorship – it will deliver 100% of the time and it gets what it gets. If you receive 500 pageviews, the ad will serve 500 impressions. This is really great and sponsorship of an area of your site is what you should be aiming at when you approach an advertiser.

Sponsorship has the highest priority level in DFP and is set as Priority 4.

- Standard: This is the default setting, and means that you set the number of impressions to deliver in a specified time frame. The ad server then tries to serve them based upon the 'Delivery impressions' you set (see below). Notice that this comes in three flavours:

    Standard: High (Priority 6)

    Standard: Normal (Priority 8)

    Standard: Low (Priority 10)

- The next four types are really meant for big ad exchange networks more than for blogs, but I'll go through them for completeness, as understanding them will help you sell the right type of package to meet your advertiser's budget. These three are based on non-guaranteed inventory. What that means is that unlike the two types above where you can guarantee complete exposure (sponsorship) or a certain number of impressions (standard), here an advertiser can have whatever is left over after the sponsored or standard items have met their daily delivery targets.

  * Network: This is where you would sell a certain percentage of the remnant inventory. After the standard items have met their daily quota, the remnant inventory will start to deliver a percentage (that you define) of the remaining impressions (assuming no sponsorship is in effect).

    Network is set as Priority 12.

  * Bulk: Here you would sell a specific number of remaining impressions, capping it at a figure that you specify. As you can't guarantee the number of remaining impressions, you sell your advertiser a cap as to what it could reach. These are delivered on a lower priority than 'Network' as the percentage rule kicks in first.

    Bulk has Priority 12.

  * Price: If you set your remaining line items with price priority then the advertiser who has paid the highest price will get priority for delivering their ad first. Again these can be set with daily or even lifetime caps to ensure everyone has an OTS (Opportunity To be Seen).

    Price is Priority 12.

  * AdSense/Ad Exchange: This obviously displays your AdSense ads, on which we'll go into greater detail in Chapter 27, which work on a different model than the other ads you should be selling since you only get paid from an AdSense ad if someone clicks on it.

    AdSense/Ad Exchange is Priority 12.

- House: Here, the lowest priority ad only displays when the DFP can't find any other ads that meet any of the parameters that you have defined. A house ad is typically one you set up to advertise your own website (or perhaps even a sister website that you own). It will replace a blank space if DFP can't find an ad.

House has the lowest priority of 16.

Line item delivery options

After you've determined the 'Type', you need to specify the 'Start time', 'End time' and the 'Quantity' of either impressions or clicks to be served. DFP from here will then calculate how many to deliver each day. You can optionally add the 'Rate' and 'Discount' to help DFP better schedule higher value ads.

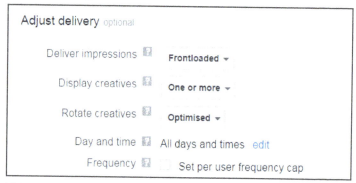

Fig 25.9 You can optionally adjust the delivery method of your line item based on certain parameters to speed up a line item delivery.

You can choose to 'Deliver impressions' based on three options:

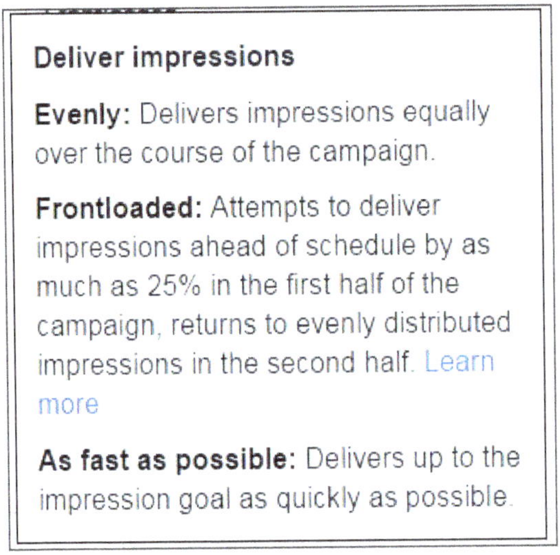

Deliver impressions

Evenly: Delivers impressions equally over the course of the campaign.

Frontloaded: Attempts to deliver impressions ahead of schedule by as much as 25% in the first half of the campaign, returns to evenly distributed impressions in the second half. Learn more

As fast as possible: Delivers up to the impression goal as quickly as possible.

Fig 25.10 The 'Deliver impressions' options are a way to override the distribution of the impressions.

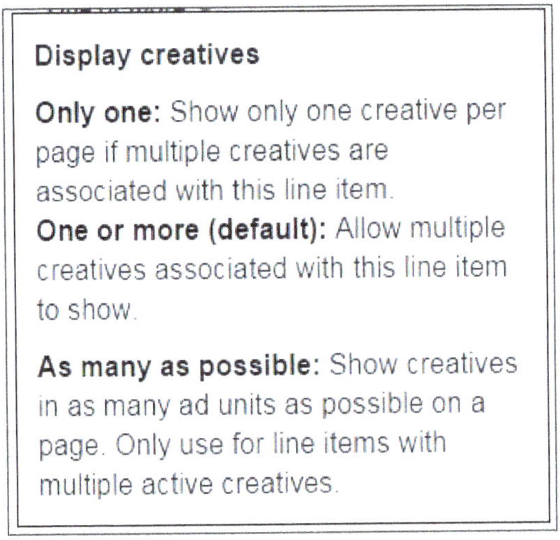

Display creatives

Only one: Show only one creative per page if multiple creatives are associated with this line item.
One or more (default): Allow multiple creatives associated with this line item to show.

As many as possible: Show creatives in as many ad units as possible on a page. Only use for line items with multiple active creatives.

Fig 25.11 When an advertiser provides you with more than one creative (e.g. a Leader Board and a MPU), you can decide whether or not to display them together on the same page or have them deliver individually.

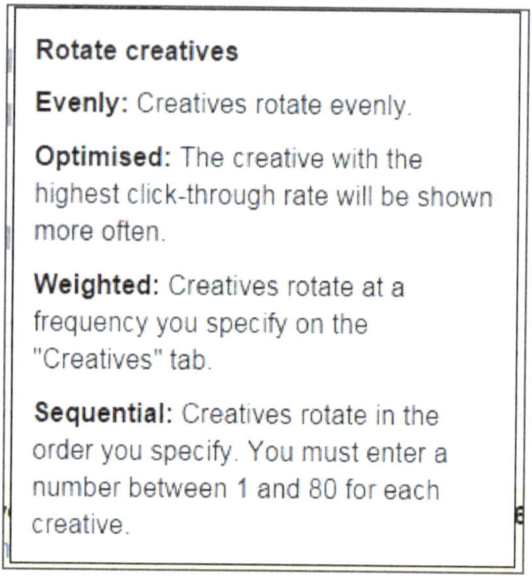

Rotate creatives
Evenly: Creatives rotate evenly.
Optimised: The creative with the highest click-through rate will be shown more often.
Weighted: Creatives rotate at a frequency you specify on the "Creatives" tab.
Sequential: Creatives rotate in the order you specify. You must enter a number between 1 and 80 for each creative.

Fig 25.12 This is more for when you have multiple creatives for the same slot, e.g. if an advertiser has provided more than one Leader Board, you can choose when each should be displayed.

Scheduling options in the line item

You can also schedule which days and time you want a line item to be delivered.

Rotate creatives
Optimised
Day and time
All days and times
edit
Frequency
Set per user frequency cap

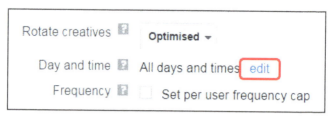

Fig 25.13 Hit 'edit' to set up a day and time schedule.

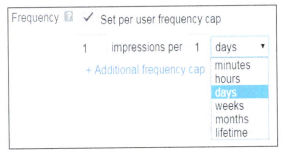

Day and time

Edit days and times that your line item will appear

Reset all days and times

Clock: 12 hour | **24 hour**

Day	Time period	0:00	4:00	8:00	12:00	16:00	20:00
Monday	Running all day						
Tuesday	Running all day						
Wednesday	Running all day						
Thursday	Running all day						
Friday	Running all day						
Saturday	Running all day						
Sunday	Running all day						

Schedule line items using   ● Publisher's time zone   User's time zone

OK   Cancel

Fig 25.14 You can then schedule the exact days and times you'd like the ads to run.

The last parameter, 'Frequency', allows you to set capping rules to cap the number of times a visitor sees the same ad (over a minute, hour, day, week, month or lifetime of the ad).

Fig 25.15 Ticking the 'Set per user frequency cap' checkbox will open up a new set of options for you to control the frequency capping of the line item.

Targeting options – how to target countries and sections of your blog

The last section in setting up your line items is about targeting your ads to certain parts of your site or to certain geographies.

Fig 25.16 You can target your ads based on custom inventory (i.e. inventory you have placed on certain sections of your site) and base it on certain geographic locations.

To sell ads on certain sections on your site, you need to create ad units (see Chapter 24) and place them in the relevant parts of your blog. These will then appear in the right side of the ad targeting inventory box.

Fig 25.17 On one of my blogs I target certain advertising to the ad units in the 3D section of my site. I create different ad units for the writing section of my site and point different line items to those ad units.

Note that you can create a placement, which is a collection of ad units together, and point your line item to it. This has the same effect as pointing to individual ad units. I find pointing to the ad units to be one level more simplified, although if you have lots of ad units on the page and multiple sections, you may consider using the ad placement option.

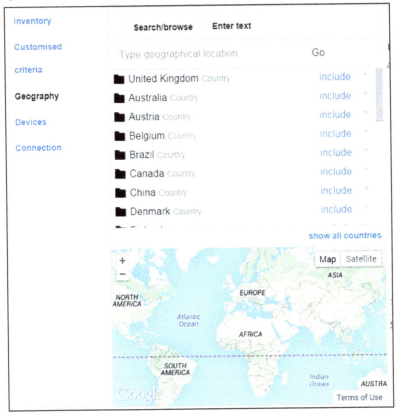

Fig 25.18 To target certain line items to particular countries, select 'Geography' and press 'include' next to the particular country you want to target.

You have now specified all the parameters around the delivery of the line item. The next step is to upload the creative(s) and check that you have enough inventory to deliver.

Fig 25.19 Click on the 'Save and...' button to expand the drop-down. From here, choose 'Upload creatives'.

Adding the creative(s) to the line item

This is the third element of the campaign, where you specify what the creative is, where it should link to and what the individual creative flight dates are. It may seem odd at first that you have to define the dates again, but it actually does make sense. For instance, the advertiser may want to reveal the first part of a message, 'New products coming soon!' between the 1st and 15th and then on the 16th to display the second ad, 'New product launches today!' and so on.

The 'Upload creatives' element allows you to add as many creatives as you like and to give them all their own individual flight dates and targets. Be sure to match the sizes in each creative's settings with the sizes you've defined in the line item size boxes.

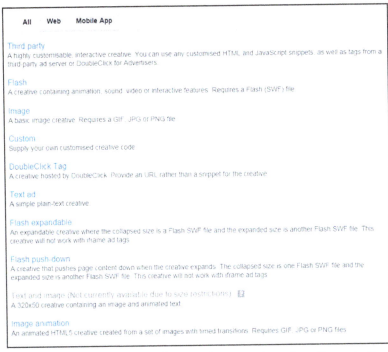

Fig 25.20 There are many types of creative elements to choose from. Most typically you will choose to upload a 'Flash', 'Image' or if you have a sophisticated advertiser, a 'Double Click Tag'.

Whichever you are given, you will still enter the same basic information.

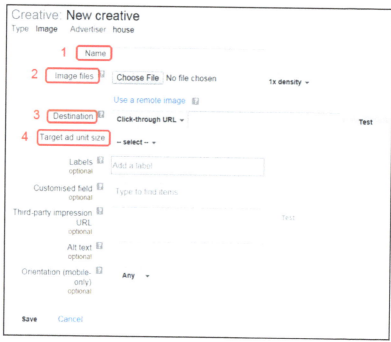

Fig 25.21 When adding a new image, you will specify its basic details. After you hit 'Save', you'll be able to define the flight dates.

Although this is very straightforward, let's quickly step through it, as there are a couple of things to note when uploading the creative.

1) Try to keep the 'Name' informative and descriptive so that you can easily see what the creative refers to. There are many different naming conventions you can use – one that I find useful is Advertiser_creativeName_adUnitSize_dateRange.

2) Hit 'Choose File' to browse to the creative the advertiser emailed you.

3) Enter the destination URL here (the whole http address) and use 'Test' to verify the link.

4) Choose the corresponding ad unit sizes that match the creative you are uploading (when done correctly, these will match one of the 'Inventory sizes' (Fig 25.6) you enter when creating the line item).

Once done, hit 'Save' and you'll be taken to the creative's settings page where you can then enter the dates that you'd like the creative to be displayed.

Fig 25.22 You can adjust the start and end times in the normal fashion by clicking on the calendar button.

To add JavaScript code is just as easy. Choose one of the creative element types (Third party, Custom, DoubleClick Tag – Fig 25.20) and then it's as simple as pasting the generated code into the text box.

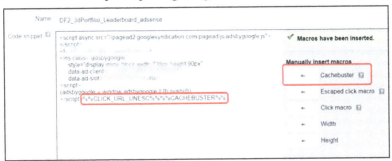

Fig 25.23 Simply paste your code into the box and DFP will then recognise it if it is from one of the main suppliers of tags (e.g. DoubleClick, FlashTalking, AdSense). Then press the arrow to the left of 'Cachebuster'. This will prevent browser caching and counting discrepancies.

When you have finished adding all your creative elements into the line item, you will be able to see them all in a list in the 'Creatives' tab at the top:

Fig 25.24 Note that you can change the 'Start time' and 'End time' by hovering the mouse over the creative and then clicking on the pencil icon (highlighted in red) to change the dates.

In this chapter you have learnt how to create an order and add line items into it. You have learnt how you can target your line items according to several different targeting criteria and how to add multiple creatives of different types into your line items. In the next chapter you will learn how to report on the delivery and clicks of your line items.

Chapter 26:

Reporting in DFP.

In this chapter, we are going to walk through the various ways in which you can report on your campaign's performance and provide your advertisers with a slew of useful metrics way above and beyond just the number of clicks they received.

There are actually two methods for accessing reports. You can either go through the main 'Reports' menu at the top or through to the individual line item to access it directly.

Site-based reporting

Let's step through each process.

Fig 26.1 The first place to access reports is in the top tab.

From here, your left-hand menu will change to reflect all the options that you would expect for reporting. These are split into six sections:

- Insights
- Saved reports
- Delivery
- Inventory
- Sales
- Reach

Fig 26.2 The 'Insights' option contains one item that will tell you about the yield of your ads.

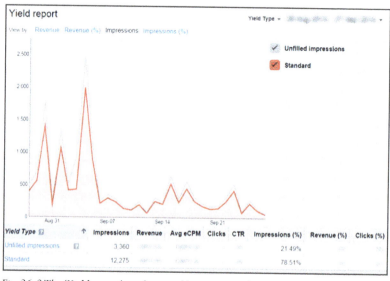

Fig 26.3 The 'Yield report' can be sorted by revenue or by impressions.

You can change the view of graph to an aggregated demand channel by clicking on the 'Yield Type' drop-down menu and choosing 'Aggregated Demand Channel'. These graphs will help you compare the performance of various ad types in a single report. If you've entered the pricing into the line item, then you can see the revenue that each ad type has brought in for you and help you realise opportunities that would be cumbersome to acquire in other reports.

The next set of reports will show you any that have been saved, shared or that you've chosen as a 'Starred' (i.e. as a favourite by using the star icon in the line item area).

> **Saved reports**
>
> Owned by me
>
> Shared with me
>
> Starred

Fig 26.4 Access reports that have been shared with you or that you have set as starred (favourited).

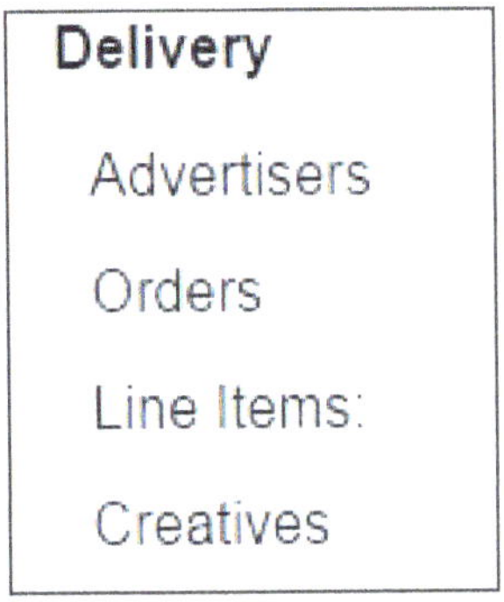

> **Delivery**
>
> Advertisers
>
> Orders
>
> Line Items:
>
> Creatives

Fig 26.5 The 'Delivery' section is where you can directly access reports based on any of the campaign setup stages we spoke about in Chapter 23.

This is actually one of the powerhouse reports, as you can now compare directly your advertisers or line items, or even go as granular as to see which creative has performed the best.

Now if you've followed my setup naming conventions (see Chapter 24), you can turbo-power these results and see which sections of your blog and which of those ad positions are performing the best.

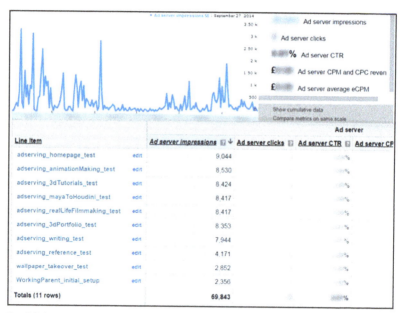

Fig 26.6 By naming my line items after the sections on my blog, I can see which levels of engagements (the column labelled 'Ad server CTR') I am receiving in each of my sections — yet another example of how a good naming convention can help you further down the line.

You can do exactly the same if you click on the creative to see the aggregated results for all your creative elements.

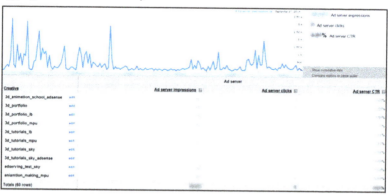

Fig 26.7 Since you are smart, you have named your creative elements with the name of the section of your blog and the ad slot that they sit in. Now you can directly compare the sections of your blog against how each creative in that section has performed.

230

Now let's move on to deal with the inventory available and how each element has performed over any given timeframe.

Fig 26.8 *This is a great place to find out which types of ads were served and interacted with. For example, if you sold ads directly or used AdSense, 'Ad units' will tell you where on the page you had the most interaction.*

The first of these reports is the 'Network' report, which breaks down your data based upon the network you want to inspect.

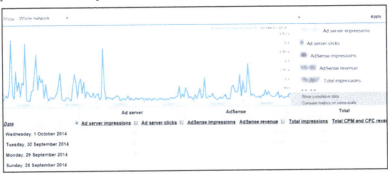

Fig 26.9 *At the top left you can select which part of the network you want to focus in on. In the centre is a graph showing performance together with any potential outliers (so that you can find out what caused those spikes and replicate it). On the right side is a summary sheet of impressions and clicks over the period and below is a table that shows daily performance of the network types.*

The next item 'Ad units' is one of my favourite report types, especially if you have named your ad units according to your site, section and position.

Ad unit		Ad server	
		Ad server impressions 🔲 ↓	Ad server CPM
DF2_MPU1	ec		
DF2_Sky	ec		
DF2_leaderboard	ec		
DF2_animationMaking_Leaderboard	ec		
DF2_wallpaper_takeover	ec		
DF2_animationMaking_MPU1	ec		
DF2_animationMaking_sky	ec		
DF2_3dTutorialsMayaToHoudiniConversionCourse_MPU1	ec		
DF2_realLifeFilmmaking_MPU1	ec		
DF2_3dTutorials_leaderboard	ec		
DF2_3dTutorials_sky	ec		
DF2_realLifeFilmmaking_sky	ec		

Fig 26.10 Follow a naming convention so you can see how your ads have performed. You can use the same convention that I use: site_section_adUnit. In this case I didn't (but I should have) use homepage for the top three ad unit names.

The other columns to the right (cropped) are 'Ad server CPM and CPC revenue', 'AdSense impressions' and 'AdSense revenue'.

'Placements' are a different way to show the ad units, grouping them together in one place, e.g. I could group all my animationMaking ad units in an animationMaking placement.

'Geography' obviously shows the Ad impressions and CPM/CPC by country.

Country	Ad server	
	Ad server impressions 🔲 ↓	Ad server CPM and CPC
United Kingdom	47,117	
United States	4,987	
Brazil	1,813	
Canada	1,335	
India	1,255	
Mexico	1,161	
Pakistan	1,145	
Taiwan	1,050	
Italy	708	

Fig 26.11 Now you can break down the ad impressions to find out how different countries are interacting with your advertising. You can then use the targeting options in the line item setup to display different ads and ad types in different countries.

'Targeting' gives you information on the browsers that people are using to access your blog, e.g. Internet Explorer 10 versus Firefox 32. If this of interest, then this is the report for you.

The last section deals with the 'AdSense' breakdown. Bear in mind that this will only work if you make your ad units available for AdSense targeting (when setting up the inventory and line item). In the following chapters I am going to walk you through AdSense and the far more granular reporting that you can get from your AdSense reporting suite.

The next section – about 'Sales' – will allow you to break your results down between 'Salespeople' and 'Advertisers'.

Fig 26.12 The reports will pick 'Salesperson' and 'Advertiser' from the setup of the 'New order'.

To set the 'Salesperson', you will need to expand the 'Optional order fields' when you set up the 'New order'.

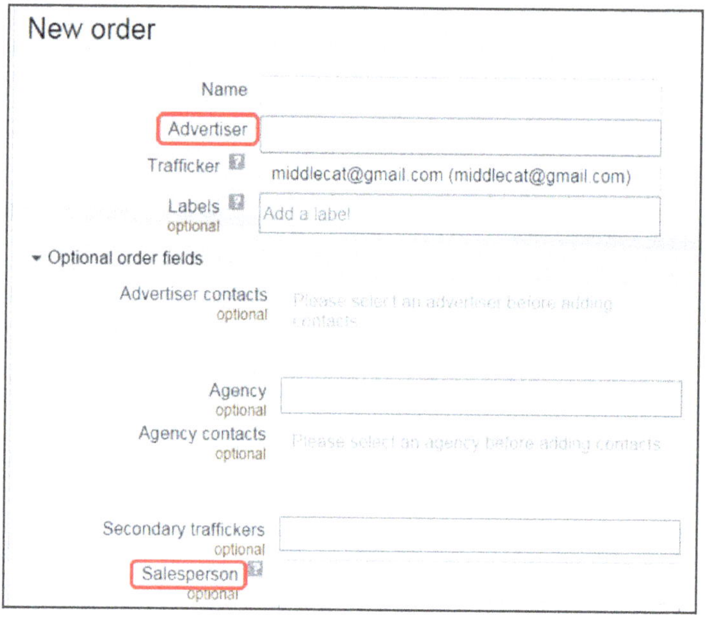

New order

Name

[Advertiser]

Trafficker   middlecat@gmail.com (middlecat@gmail.com)

Labels
optional   Add a label

▼ Optional order fields

Advertiser contacts
optional   Please select an advertiser before adding contacts

Agency
optional

Agency contacts
optional   Please select an agency before adding contacts

Secondary traffickers
optional

[Salesperson]
optional

Fig 26.13 It may take a bit longer, but by filling in as much detail at the start of the 'New order' as possible, you can start to get far more granular reporting on the performance of the 'Salesperson'.

The next section is a very interesting section that has reports on the reach of your advertising.

Reach

Network

Advertisers

Orders

Line Items:

Ad units

Fig 26.14 'Reach' reports help you determine the number of unique visitors exposed to any of the menu items listed.

Let's step through these to see how valuable this information can be in terms of showing potential advertisers just how their advertising could 'reach' an audience in a way that would be impossible for print advertising to demonstrate.

Show Active ad units ▼	▼		Apply
Ad server impressions 🔲		Unique visitors	🔲
45,763		-	

Month and year	Ad server	Reach
	Ad server impressions 🔲 ↓	Unique visitors 🔲
May 2014	13,771	51
September 2014	10,321	130
August 2014	9,625	79
June 2014	7,362	121
July 2014	4,684	57
Totals (5 rows)	45,763	-

Fig 26.15 You can now see the number of impressions and unique visitors that the advertising reached in each month. Note that by default it's ordered in terms of 'Ad server impressions'. Click on the 'Month and year' heading to order it chronologically. Clicking on any of the particular months will show you what happened on each day within that month.

The 'Advertisers' report will give you the same 'Reach' data, but this time ordered by the different advertisers you have enlisted. The same is true of 'Orders', which will list the results in terms of orders placed.

I want to show you the value of the 'Line items' and 'Ad units' reports, which when used in conjunction with the naming conventions I've shown you in Chapter 25, will yield some very deep insights and help you sell advertising to the right advertiser in the right section.

Firstly, you can break down the 'Ad server impressions' and 'Unique visitors' per line item.

Line Item	Ad server Ad server impressions	Reach Unique visitors
adserving_3dTutorials_test	5,232	176
adserving_animationMaking_test	5,232	175
adserving_homepage_test	5,232	176
adserving_mayaToHoudini_test	5,232	177
adserving_realLifeFilmmaking_test	5,232	177
adserving_writing_test	5,232	193
adserving_3dPortfolio_test	5,231	179
adserving_reference_test	4,318	288
WorkingParent_initial_setup	2,434	154
wallpaper_takeover_test	1,744	175
df2_digital_adserving	1,482	124
Totals (11 rows)	46,601	-

Ad server impressions: **46,601** Unique visitors: **-**

Fig 26.16 By creating and naming separate ad units and line items for each of the sections of your blog, you can compare each line item's (i.e. each section's) advertising reach.

The 'Ad units' report does the same, but this time you can break it down per ad unit.

	Ad server	Reach
Ad unit / Month and year	Ad server impressions	Unique visitors
DF2_3dPortfolio_leader	840	-
May 2014	564	60
June 2014	276	121
DF2_3dPortfolio_sky	840	-
May 2014	564	60
June 2014	276	121
DF2_3dTutorials_leaderboard	840	-
May 2014	564	60
June 2014	276	121
DF2_3dTutorials_MPU1	840	-
May 2014	564	60
June 2014	276	121
DF2_3dTutorials_sky	840	-

Fig 26.17 You can take this concept one step further and now determine the reach of each ad unit within each section.

How to choose the metrics and dimensions in your report

You may have noticed that the default reports show 'Ad server impressions' and 'Unique visitors'. You may quite rightly wonder how it is possible for you to see metrics such as click-throughs and CTRs. To do this, click on the 'edit report' link at the top of any of the report screens.

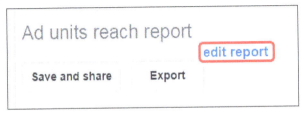

Fig 26.18 Clicking on 'edit report' will allow you to add custom rows and columns to display any given dimension and metric.

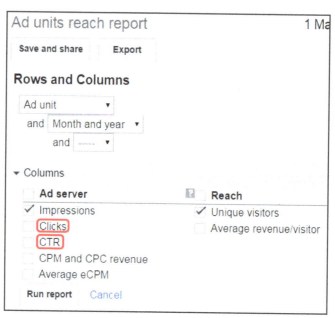

Fig 26.19 As you can see, 'Impressions' and 'Unique visitors' were clicked on by default. If you want to add 'Clicks' and 'CTR', just tick their checkboxes and hit 'Run report'.

Reporting on an individual campaign

All these reporting tools are great in terms of reporting on the overall performance of the advertising on the blog, but what you will be asked mostly by an advertiser is 'How has their individual campaign performed?', i.e. the campaign that you sold them.

This by default isn't in the reporting section, but it is actually very simple to find this out. Go into the line item in question and you will see a 'Run report' link to the right of the top buttons.

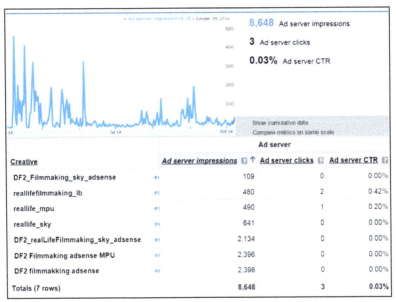

Line Item adserving_realLifeFilmmaking_test · Delivering

Standard 7 Apr 2014 00 00 BST - 30 Apr 2016 23 59 BST

Pause   Add creatives   More actions ▾   Run report

Impressions   Clicks   CTR   Progress
8,648   3   0.03% 104%

Fig 26.20 In the header of each line item you will see a performance snapshot and the progress bar on the right is particularly interesting, with the vertical line showing how far into the flight dates the campaign has progressed (this one is still quite early). As the line item progresses, the vertical line will move further to the right, the green area showing how far ahead (it would be a green bar) or behind (it would be a red bar) the delivery target the line item currently is.

When you run the report, you will be able to see the delivery activity and breakdown of each of the creative(s) within that line item.

Creative		Ad server impressions	Ad server clicks	Ad server CTR
DF2_Filmmaking_sky_adsense	e	109	0	0.00%
reallifefilmmaking_lb	e	480	2	0.42%
reallife_mpu	e	490	1	0.20%
reallife_sky	e	641	0	0.00%
DF2_realLifeFilmmaking_sky_adsense	e	2,134	0	0.00%
DF2 Filmmaking adsense MPU	e	2,396	0	0.00%
DF2 filmmakking adsense	e	2,398	0	0.00%
Totals (7 rows)		8,648	3	0.03%

8,648 Ad server impressions

3 Ad server clicks

0.03% Ad server CTR

Fig 26.21 Running the report gives a graphical summary of the delivery activity and how each line item performed within the reporting period.You can mouse over any point on the graph and see how many impressions were served on that date.

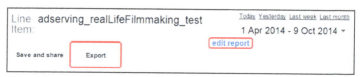

Fig 26.22 You can edit the report in the same way as in Fig 26.18 and Fig 26.19, and also have the option to 'Export' the report to send to your sponsors.

Fig 26.23 After hitting 'Export', a pop-up window will appear. The options here are fairly rudimentary but essentially you can choose the format to save the report in. For most clients an 'XLS' or 'XLSX' will suffice.

The report will then be downloaded to your download folders. A practice that I often use is to rename it to the name of:

- Your blog – this is useful both to your advertiser as they can see instantly in their system which blog this relates to, and is also useful for you if/when you have multiple blogs.

- Your advertiser – to quickly identify who it is.

- The individual line item – because an advertiser may have more than one line item booking with you.

- The date – if an advertiser books for longer periods they may want a monthly report or a report to show the activity for a certain creative, e.g. they may have campaign for an event or show to which your blog may be driving traffic.

Have your folder architecture on your own drive reflect these naming conventions, otherwise you run the risk of having reports sporadically strewn around your download folder or plastered across the desktop.

Another thing that I do is to take a screen grab of the results screen (Fig 26.21) and include that in the email, also writing a sentence or two on how well the campaign performed for the advertiser.

Obviously be judicious about when you do this, if the campaign performed badly then there's no harm in sending a basic report on its own. The techniques we've learnt up to this point will help you understand why the line item would have performed poorly and more importantly what you can do to ensure that this doesn't happen again.

So now you are pretty well-armed in both Analytics and ad serving, and can make the most of your blog's potential. There is, however, another element that you may wish to consider while you try to find advertising partners. This element is ad exchanges and ad networks. Do you need them and indeed would any of these be helpful in your blogging journey? In the next section, we'll walk through the various ad exchanges and networks and assess which of these (and indeed whether any of these) would be a good fit for your blog.

Part 6:

Ad networks, Ad exchanges
and
your blog

Chapter 27:

Does your blog need an ad network/ exchange platform?

You may wonder (and you'd be quite correct to) why exactly you would need to use an ad network for your blog. After all, the whole focus – indeed the holy grail of this book thus far – has been about getting a partner to sponsor your blog. That is absolutely true and should remain your aim. However, there may be a place for ad networks for a few reasons:

a) Ad network ads can help fill a void if you haven't sold all your inventory, e.g. if Advertiser A buys all the Leader Boards on you site and Advertiser B buys 10,000 MPU impressions, an ad network can help fill the blank spaces on your blog.

b) While you are acquiring advertisers, ad network ads can help you assess what value to put on your advertising slots, e.g. you may find you are making £300 a month from the Leader Board ad and £100 from the Sky through the ad network – this will help you price your inventory at the correct value.

c) You will be collecting valuable data that can help you broker a deal that is in both your and the advertiser's best interests. You will be better able to manage the advertiser's expectations if you know what your average engagement levels are (e.g. CTR or mouse rollovers in the case of expandable banner ads) and based on the ad network performance you will know whether an advertiser's campaign has been a success or not.

Essentially an ad network would be able to fill any remnant inventory you may have on your blog. The percentage of remnant inventory will vary; it's quite likely at the start that you may have 100% remnant inventory while you find and negotiate a deal with an advertiser.

What an ad network can do is to fill that void, providing relevant ads for your audience. Having relevant ads served in the correct quantity to your audience will help you to monetise your content most efficiently.

You may wonder why you would spend so much time and energy trying to find a direct advertiser when an ad network (for example Google AdSense) can serve relevant ads. This is a good question. Think of it in this way: as your blog evolves, the choice you make between direct advertising and using ad networks will swing back and forth. Knowing how to blend the two types of advertising gives your blog incredible agility to meet the challenges of your blogging journey.

Having a direct advertiser ultimately means that you control who is advertising on your blog. Using the methods I have presented, you can identify and cherry pick the right advertiser for you. Ultimately you don't have to share the revenue with anyone else because depending upon the particular ad network you choose, you may receive up to 70% of the click share. And that's the key thing here – when you negotiate directly with your advertiser using your analytics reports and give them compelling reasons to buy advertising on your blog, you should be aiming to sell on a CPM or sponsorship model. This means that you will get paid regardless of whether anyone clicks on the adverts or not (although obviously if no one clicks, then your relationship with the advertiser will be short-lived).

On the other hand, ad networks and ad exchanges will generally only pay you if someone clicks on any particular ad. This means that if you get a 1% CTR then you'd only get paid for that 1%, and even then you'd only get a share of that (1% CTR) revenue. In this case, you have allowed 99% of advertisers to advertise for free on your site.

But if ad networks and exchanges are so inefficient, then why are you reading (and why am I writing) a chapter on the section? It's quite simple. You can implement an ad network and have ads running on your site in minutes. This means you can start to use and assess your blog's advertising potential instantaneously, allowing you to get on with the business of blogging and building your audience until you identify, contact and negotiate with an advertiser to buy directly from your blog.

One of the most popular is Google AdSense, a service that will crawl through your blog, analysing your content and displaying relevant advertising.

What does 'relevant advertising' mean? Well it comes in two flavours:

- Contextual advertising – This means the ad network/exchange will serve ads that match the content of your blog. If you're blogging about fast cars, you'll see ads appear from advertisers in the automotive space. These could be from multiple advertisers who you wouldn't necessarily be able to forge a relationship with – AdSense will do the buying and selling on your behalf.

- Behavioural – This means that ads are displayed based on the visitor's browsing history. For example, if a visitor has been looking at holiday deals in the south of Spain, then holiday offers in the south of Spain will appear on your blog about fast cars (even though a blog about cars has nothing to do with holidays).

What are ad exchanges and ad networks and how do they work?

Well you may have heard of ad exchanges and ad networks and wondered what the difference between them is and which one you need to implement on your blog.

Basically, either of these two options is a fast way to match advertising to your blog. The way in which they work is that the advertiser – let's say a garden centre – will go to the ad network or exchange and ask to advertise on sites about gardening. Now imagine how long it would take you to identify the right advertiser for your blog; it will take the advertiser almost ten times longer to identify the right site on which to advertise. What ad networks and exchanges do is to find the right sites and blogs for the advertiser to place their ads on.

The garden centre advertiser now can choose to advertise across a range of gardening sites and blogs without having to contact and negotiate with each site owner and blogger. This is a seemingly win-win situation for both blogger and advertiser. The truth of the matter is that it is now an open marketplace and the exact circumstances at the instant someone lands on your blog will determine which advertiser gets the advertising placement for that visitor.

Now if you factor in that there are multiple gardening advertisers and multiple gardening blogs out there, and you will start to see why for the ad networks and exchanges this is a definite win. On top of this, since all parties have signed up to the Google advertising network programmes (AdSense for publishers and AdWords for advertisers), then there is no brokering or negotiating of contracts to be done – it's just a simple box to click to accept the terms and conditions.

So then why not just have your ads powered by these networks and exchanges, rather than going alone and negotiating your own deal?

Although it's seemingly a win-win situation for advertiser and publisher, you will need to consider the fact that ad networks and exchanges do take a share of the money and by the time they taken their cut, you will be left with only a proportion of what the advertiser paid.

The second drawback is that many of these campaigns are run on a Pay Per Click (PPC) model, which means that you will only receive revenue whenever a visitor clicks on an ad. Now that kind of works against every other form of advertising model out there – neither radio, TV or billboard advertising, the radio station doesn't get paid if the listener buys the product. PPC does work well for advertisers, ad exchanges and ad networks, but although it's in their interests, it's not so great for you (the blogger then spends her time watching her AdSense account to see if someone has clicked, rather than getting on with blogging).

As we've mentioned, these methods are fast and easy, and in the next couple of chapters I'll show you how to set up and implement ads through Google AdSense (although there are many other ad networks and exchanges, some who pay better rates than AdSense, Google AdSense is one of the most used and very fast to implement on your blog). You'll also find out how you can make specific sections of your blog targetable to certain advertisers and how you can exclude particular ads from appearing on your site. This will allow you to present targeted adverts which are relevant to your audience's interests.

Chapter 28:

Setting up Google AdSense on your blog.

The setting up of Google AdSense is relatively straightforward. What you'll be doing is setting up an account (if you've got this far, you are most likely well-bedded into the Google ecosystem) and creating the equivalent of line items to target particular advertisers to certain sections of your blog. Although the algorithms that AdSense run are so advanced now that this step may be redundant, it is still extremely valuable to do this, since you can widen the scope of potential advertisers for different areas of your blog. It will also turbo-charge the insights you get in the reporting section.

Fig 28.1 The layout is similar to other Google products. On the top left you can access the main sections of the product and on the top right you can access your user settings.

You can see that there are four main parts to AdSense:

- Home – This is where you can see a summary of all your activity, including:
    * earnings today, yesterday, over the last seven days and over the last 28 days
    * current balance
    * performance of your ad units
        ▪ page views
        ▪ top channels (I'll show you how to create custom channels)

- top sites (again I'll show you how to deploy ads from an AdSense account to multiple blogs and sites)

- top countries

- top platforms (i.e. desktop, high end mobile devices and tablets)

- My Ads – This is where you will create your ad units to correspond to the ad unit sizes you have on your blog, create bespoke custom channels so your ad units are visible to particular advertisers for different sections of your blogs or even over multiple blogs.

- Allow & block ads – You may not want certain advertisers, ad networks or areas of advertising to appear on your blog (e.g. gambling or dating sites), so this is the area in which you can determine who doesn't appear on your blog.

- Performance reports – There are many different reports that you can generate from here. Don't worry – we'll step through them all.

Let's start with the 'Home' page.

The 'Home' screen is essentially a set of dashboards that will give you an at-a-glance view of what is happening on your AdSense ads. A great feature of this dashboard is that it puts the figures into context, i.e. it shows a trend of what is happening over four time periods: today, yesterday, the last 7 days and the last 28 days.

Fig 28.2 Right at the top of the 'Home' screen you will see how your AdSense ads are performing across four time periods. This is much more useful than any single number, as you can create a context for the figures. You can of course go into further detail in the performance reports, but as a dashboard this is a very effective method to display the data.

Fig 28.3 The next items show your current balance, i.e. what is owed to you at the moment. You may have already received money, so this is the outstanding balanced owed. The scorecard provides a handy summary of how well-optimised your blog is for AdSense and clicking on any of the headings here will provide you with help for the pages that need further optimising.

Payment thresholds in Google AdSense

Note that there is a threshold that AdSense sets before you will receive payment for the ads. These thresholds vary depending upon the currency you are using and your payment method.

Thresholds	Tax Information Entry	Address Verification	Form of Payment Entry	Payment	Cancellation
US Dollar (USD)	$0	$10	$10	$100	$10
Euro (EUR)	N/A	€10	€10	€70	€10
Great British Pound (GBP)	N/A	£10	£10	£60	£10
Australian Dollar (AUD)	N/A	A$15	A$15	A$100	A$15
Canadian Dollar (CAD)	C$0	C$10	C$10	C$100	C$10
Czech Koruna (CZK)	N/A	Kč200	Kč200	Kč2,000	Kč200
Danish Krone (DKK)	N/A	kr60	kr60	kr600	kr60
Hong Kong Dollar (HKD)	N/A	HK$100	HK$100	HK$800	HK$100

Fig 28.4 The payment threshold seems to be around the 10 mark for most currencies or the equivalent of what would otherwise be the $10 mark. AdSense will send you a PIN in the mail (snail mail) to verify your postal address and you can only receive payment when you enter this PIN (full instructions are in the envelope they send you).

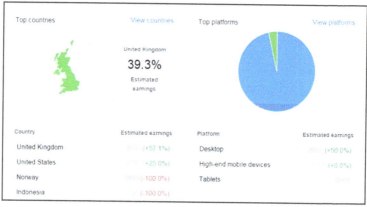

Fig 28.5 At the bottom of the homepage are the reports for the 'Top Countries' and 'Top platforms'. The blue links in the top right corners of each of these widgets take you directly to the full report for each item.

Useful Google add-ons

Interestingly enough, right at the bottom of the 'Home' section are links to other AdSense products. The most interesting one is the second item – 'Publisher Toolbar' – which installs an add-on to your browser, giving you real-time information on the advertiser who is currently being displayed in your AdSense unit.

Fig 28.6 Installing the 'Publisher Toolbar' (second item) into Chrome will give you instant details about AdSense units live on your page and you can also chose to install the app on your phone. The best thing about installing the app on your phone is that you can always see how your AdSense units are performing, although it's also true that the worst thing about installing the app on your phone is that you can always see how

your AdSense units are performing!

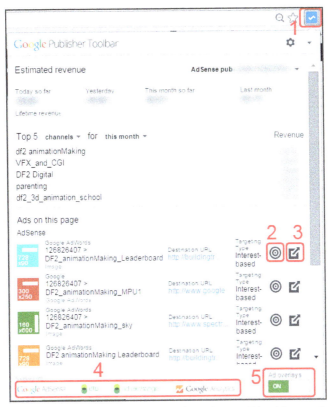

Fig 28.7 *Once the toolbar is installed (into Chrome) you will be able to see live stats on the page's ad units that are currently displaying.*

There are a lot of very interesting features within this toolbar:

1) Accesses the toolbar through the blue icon in the top pane of Chrome. At the top you can see the current highlights as you'd see in the 'Home' page of your AdSense account.

2) Identifies the ad on your page. The page will scroll (down if necessary) to find and highlight the ad.

3) Identifies the ad and loads its details in a separate window.

4) Here you can choose to sign into any of your other Google properties to see live statistics in the toolbar.

5) Turns 'On' or 'Off' Ad overlays (see below).

Fig 28.8 With 'Ad overlays' enabled, you will see a green overlay on your AdSense ads. When you mouse over the ad unit, information about its size, the ad network and the advertiser (blue outlined box in the top left corner) is displayed.

In this section you have learnt about the home dashboard in Google AdSense, where you can find information about ad delivery and plugins where you can view AdSense information directly in your browser's toolbar. You've seen how to implement handy extensions directly into the browser, time-saving features which will give you live insight into how your page is performing across Google Analytics, DFP and AdSense. In the next section we will go through the steps of creating your ad units and you'll learn how to target particular advertisers.

Chapter 29:

Creating AdSense units and targeting advertisers.

Now you have AdSense set up, let's look into the menu item area 'My ads', where you will create, configure and target ad units to drop into your site.

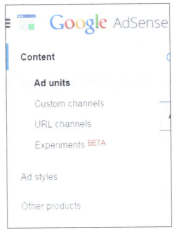

Fig 29.1 The 'My Ads' menu will allow you to configure and target your ad units to channels that you define to fit your content.

The first thing you're going to need to do is to create a new ad unit. You'll see a button right at the top that will let you do this.

Fig 29.2 Here you can create a new ad unit by hitting the button on the left and import old ad code (if you have any). On the far right, you can start to filter through your results to bring up, say, only Leader Boards or only ads targeted to a certain part of your blog.

Pressing the '+ New ad unit' button will take you to a new screen where you can start to build the ad unit.

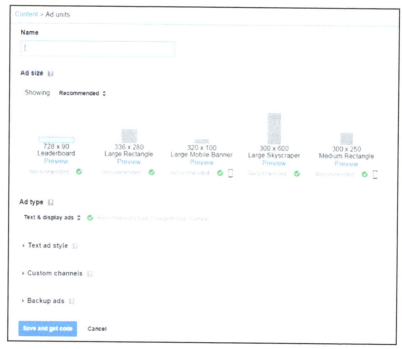

Fig 29.3 The simple wizard-style layout will help you to quickly build up your ad units.

A couple of things here to note. Firstly, when deciding upon a name, stick to a naming convention that you understand and can stay consistent with. An excellent convention is to base your ad units using:

- blogName_blogSection_AdUnitSize

This convention will allow you to find and edit ad units very quickly. For example, if you run two blogs about cars (let's say a luxury car blog and a second-hand car blog) which have several different advertisers, you could have ad unit names like:

- luxuryCarBlog_retroCars_mpu
- luxuryCarBlog_modernCars_leaderboard
- secondHandCar_sellingCars_skyscraper

If you can come up with another convention that works for you, then go for that one; the important thing is to stick with a unified naming convention. Spending a bit of time at the start getting your naming convention working will save you getting into a terrible mess further down the line as your blog(s) grow.

Ad sizes and formats

You'll notice too that the ad sizes displayed may not match the ones on your blog. This is because these are the recommendations based across the range of formats.

Fig 29.4 To find the precise size you want, click on the 'Showing' drop-down menu to access the format type you need.

Fig 29.5 The same thing is true of the 'Ad type' — click on the drop-down to switch between 'Display' or 'Text' ads or have them both (default).

The next part is for text-only ads where you can define your colour palette.

Fig 29.6 Here you can style your ad to match the colours of your blog design. Be careful not to go too wild on the style – the aim is to get people to click on your ads, not to turn them off! The closer you match this colour template to your blog's, the better the ads will sit in the page. Alternatively, you could use contrasting colours to make the ads stand out. As always, there's no one-size-fits-all rule – experiment with different setups and see what works for your blog.

Creating targeted channels to find the right advertiser

The next part is the real powerhouse of the system, where you can start to create custom channels for your ad units. Being able to create custom channels is such a powerful feature and is what makes this a really viable option for generating advertising revenue for your blog. Let's take some time out to explore why this is.

I'll use one of my own blogs as an example. On www.digitopiafilm. com I have four distinct areas: 'animation making', 'filmmaking', 'writing' and '3D tutorials'. I'd like to target the advertising for each of these areas to different advertisers, e.g. I'd like to match the advertising up such that:

- 3D animation software ad units appear on the 'animation making' part
- film schools ad units appear on the 'filmmaking' part
- writing software and services ad units appear on the 'writing' part
- 3D animation and VFX schools ad units appear on the '3D tutorials' part

The ability to create a custom channel in AdSense facilitates this. I can now create a set of ad units (in my case a Leader Board, MPU and Sky) across each of these areas to target individual advertisers to that part of the blog. I can then repeat this process across different blogs within the same AdSense account, allowing me to monitor the progress of each of these in one place.

There are a few ways in which this can be done, create the custom channels before, after or while creating ad units.

Fig 29.7 You can make a custom channel before creating your ad units from the menu on the left and then apply them to your ad unit, or you can use the 'Create new custom channel' button within the main body.

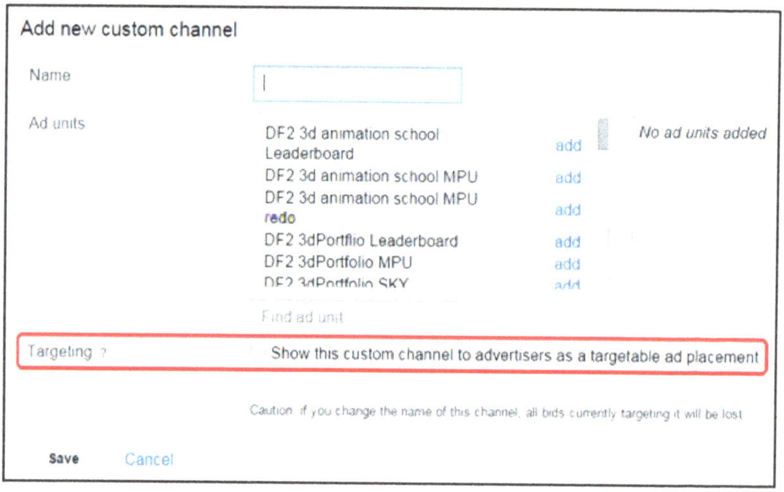

Fig 29.8 The 'Targeting' option within the 'Add new custom channel' dialogue box will allow you to target this channel (and ad units you apply this channel to) to specific advertisers.

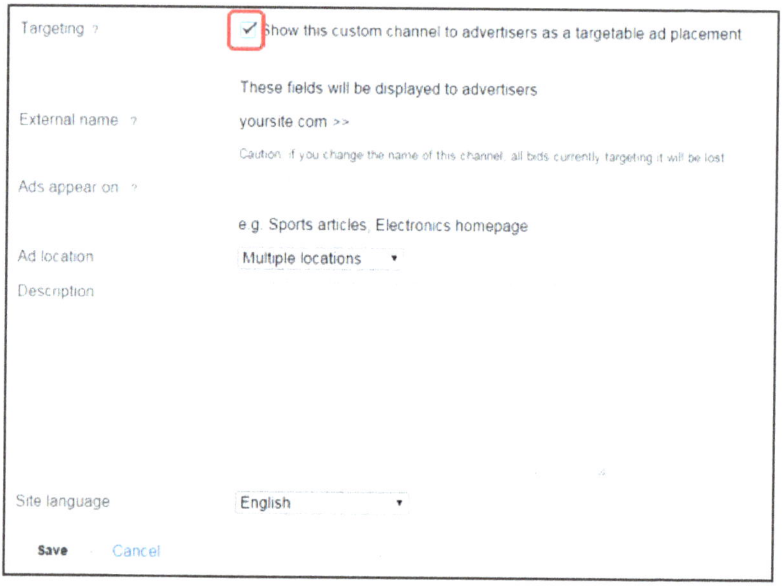

Fig 29.9 When you click on the 'Show this custom channel to advertisers as a targetable ad placement' checkbox, a set of new fields will appear, into which you now enter the targeting descriptions that will become visible to advertisers.

In these boxes you can start to describe your site and ideally your audience to the advertiser.

	These fields will be displayed to advertisers
External name ?	yoursite.com >> animation articles and animation tutorials. Top center
	Caution: if you change the name of this channel, all bids currently targeting it will be lost
Ads appear on ?	animation articles and anim
	e.g. Sports articles; Electronics homepage
Ad location	Top centre ▼
Description	For advertisers of 3D animation. CGI and VFX animationmentor, digitalTutors. Visitors here are interested in 3D CGI animation, 3D modelling and VFX. Software of interest Maya, Houdini, Realflow, ZBrush, Nuke, Modo, The Foundry, Mudbox etc

Fig 29.10 Here is an example of one of my custom targetable channels and yes, I did get AdSense adverts from all these animation schools and software vendors appearing on my blog in the animation section. Now imagine how much work it would have taken to approach all these advertisers individually. Using AdSense, I was able to get their ads to appear on my blog and my visitors engaged quickly and easily.

Remember that your advertisers are taking out AdWords campaigns. AdWords works in the opposite way to AdSense, i.e. an advertiser would take out an AdWords campaign to target a publisher who is using AdSense. So why shouldn't that publisher be you?

Once you've fully populated the fields, it's time to save the ad unit and get the ad unit code.

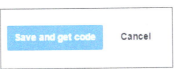

Fig 29.11 Rather than putting the code directly into your blog, we are going to put the code back into DFP.

At this point, it's much better to serve the code through your DFP account. This is because you can now start to use AdSense as a lower priority or even a house line item to run alongside your paid-for campaigns. This method will work even if you don't have any paid-for campaigns, because if the only line item you have in DFP is a low priority or house ad, it has nothing to compete against and serve. As soon as you get a paid-for campaign, it will supersede the AdSense campaign and deliver first.

For example, if you sell a 10,000 impression campaign, and you have 12,000 ad impressions a month, that means your 10,000 paid-for campaigns will run alongside (but at a higher priority) than your AdSense campaign, which will make up the difference. Unless you have a house ad, you may be best serving the AdSense ad as a house ad to make sure your paid campaigns deliver first.

Serving AdSense ads also has an excellent side benefit in that you will start to see other advertisers appearing on your site that you had not yet considered. Think of these advertisers as potential advertisers. Clearly they are spending money on AdWords, which means that they may be receptive to hearing directly from bloggers who are carrying their ads. You could probably broker a better deal directly with them, so long as you have the audience they want (and your analytics will prove this to them). As well as providing an additional revenue stream, use this as valuable, free market research on advertising opportunities.

Using the 'Custom channels' link on the left-hand menu, you can see the complete list of all the custom channels you have created:

Actions ▾				
Name ↑	ID	Status	Description	Targetable
3d animation school		Active	For advertisers of 3D animation, CGI and	Yes
View report			VFX animationmentor, digitalTutors Vis...	

Fig 29.12 Under each custom channel is a 'View report' option, which will take you to the corresponding report in the 'Performance reports' area.

In this chapter you've seen how to create ad units and add customised channels. This is a very powerful feature in creating your own targeted advertising. And you can now have the correct advertiser displaying in the corresponding part of your blog. When the advertising is relevant to the reader's interest and search intent, you give yourself a much higher probability of gaining a click, which in turn will get you higher advertising revenue.

In the next chapters, you will learn how to allow and block certain advertisers from appearing on your blogs, before going on to see how you can report on your ad units.

Chapter 30:

How to block advertisers from appearing on your blog.

The next menu item, 'Allow & block ads', will help you complete the setup of your ads. As the name suggests, this is the area where you can prevent certain advertisers from appearing.

Fig 30.1 There are several ways in which you can identify which advertisers you do and don't want to appear on your site. Being able to categorise them into broad areas will save you time.

The first item, 'Advertiser URLs', is the area in which you can individually type an advertiser's display or destination URL to block.

Fig 30.2 Blocking individual URLs is useful for blocking competitors' advertising, which may otherwise appear on your blog.

Remember that you are not allowed to click on ads to see their URLs. Instead use the Google Publishers Toolbar (that we saw in the previous chapter) to establish which URL to block.

You can block whole sites, parts of sites or individual pages. For example, you could block:

myCompetitor.com → This would block the whole of the competitor's site.

myCompetitor.com/homepage → This would only block the homepage of the competitor's site.

jobs.myCompetitor.com → This would block the 'jobs' subdomain of the competitor's site.

Now let's see how to block certain broad categories of ads from appearing on your blog.

Advertiser URLs	General categories	Sensitive categories	Ad networks	Ad serving	Ads (Ad review centre)

Use this page to allow or block general categories of ads (in any of these supported languages) from appearing on your site. ?

All categories   0 Blocked categories (50 remaining)

Allowed or blocked	Category name ↑	% Ad Impressions (last 30 days)	% Earnings (last 30 days)	Number of Blocked Sub-Categories
✔ Allowed	Apparel (8) ▶ (?)	--	--	0 / 8
✔ Allowed	Arts & Entertainment (17) ▶ (?)	0.3%	6.6%	0 / 17
✔ Allowed	Beauty & Personal Care (12) ▶ (?)	--	--	0 / 12
✔ Allowed	Business & Industrial (21) ▶ (?)	1.7%	6.8%	0 / 21
✔ Allowed	Computers & Consumer Electronics (22) ▶ (?)	4.9%	22.0%	0 / 22

Fig 30.3 Sliding the 'Allowed or blocked' bar to the left will block a certain category.

What's interesting here is that you can see which categories have actually appeared (third column – % Ad Impressions) and how much they have brought in terms of revenue (fourth column – % Earnings). This is a really good indicator of three things:

How well AdSense is contextually matching the ad units to the content of the page, i.e. in the example above 'Computers & Consumer Electronics'-based ads have appeared 4.9% of the time, bringing in 22% of the last 30 days' revenue. Ideally you would want to have that 4.9% ad impression rate higher, since it's clearly working for your audience. There are 22 categories of ads in AdSense, so you need to go through the list to check whether there are some exceptionally well-performing items. Going further down this list, I can see that 'Hobbies & Leisure' earnings massively overperforms based on the % Ad Impressions.

Fig 30.4 'Hobbies & Leisure' only accounted for 0.8% of impressions but 15.8 of earnings – logic tells us that if the ad impressions here were boosted, so too would be the number of clicks (and the advertising revenue).

- Potential advertising categories that you may have initially overlooked. There may be categories that you hadn't considered that are actually performing very well. This area shows you how well all the categories are performing, in which categories advertisers are purchasing inventory (% Ad Impressions) and how visitors are engaging with that advertising (% Earnings).

- Unrelated and underperforming ads. For instance, if certain categories are repeatedly appearing on your site that you deem unrelated, you can block these from appearing and thus free space for categories that you do want. If 'Personal Care' has a high Impression %, it is taking inventory away from relevant categories (e.g. 'Business & Industrial') and you can set its slider to 'Blocked'. By taking out unwanted categories, there will be more opportunities for the categories that you do want to appear.

Blocking sensitive categories

The next section, 'Sensitive Categories', works in exactly the same way. You can set 'Allowed' or 'Blocked' to the category and see its impressions and earnings over the last 30 days.

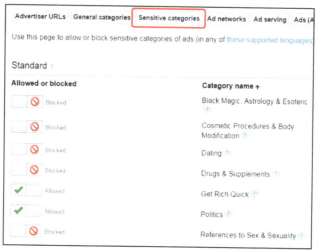

Fig 30.5 'Sensitive categories' come in two types. Here is a list of the 'Standard' categories.

Fig 30.6 The 'Restricted categories' are based on restrictions that some regions have on the types of gambling ads that display. Unless you are running a gambling and betting blog, the best thing really would be to just block these types of ads altogether.

Fig 30.7 'Ad networks' shows you list of networks who are purchasing advertising through AdSense. Unless you have a specific reason to block one of them, it's best to leave them on. Note that you don't see '% Ad Impressions' and '% Earnings' in this view.

Fig 30.8 'Ad serving' allows you to display ads based on their context. Bear in mind that if you turn off a particular type of ad, it will affect all the ad units on your page. If you don't want a social ad in a MPU slot, turning off 'Social ads' will turn that off across all your advertising units (including the MPU).

The Ad review centre

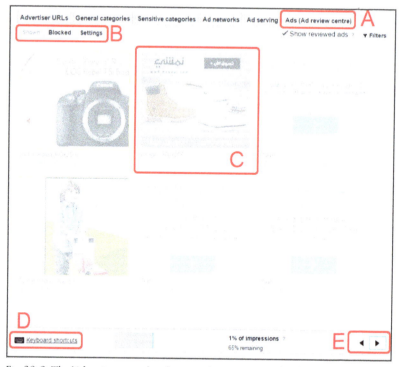

Fig 30.9 The 'Ad review centre' is the area where you can individually go through and review which ads to allow or block.

There are five areas of interest here that make this an especially powerful part of the AdSense feature set:

A   The 'Ad review centre' tab.

B   Here you can switch between the views to see which are showing, which you choose to block and the general settings, which allows you to run the ads immediately or to hold targeted ads for 24 hours for review.

C   When you mouse over the ad, its options and details will appear.

Fig 30.10 When you mouse over the ad, you can see the creative, its size, where it's pointing to and find related ads.You can also block it by pressing in the lower left corner (you are able to toggle back and forth using this button).

D   There's a selection of keyboard shortcuts that you can use to speed up the review process:

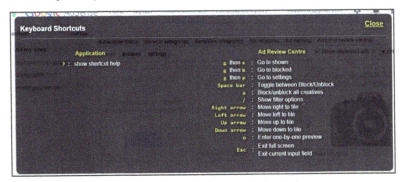

Fig 30.11 Speed up the review of your ads by using keyboard shortcuts.

E   Lets you go to the previous and next pages of ads to review.

The AdSense algorithm is already smart enough to match advertising against your post. In the last two chapters you have learnt to complement AdSense's native algorithms by creating custom channels to reach out to advertisers, how to review (allow and block) individual ads and to be super precise on the type of advertising that will appear on your blog. Using these controls enables you to fine-tune your advertising.

In the next chapter, we are going to look at the extensive reporting suite of tools within AdSense, the purpose of which is to tell you what is working so that you can filter and fine-tune your advertising even further to get results and work towards the revenue you are aiming for.

Chapter 31:

Using the AdSense reporting suite.

As you've seen already, AdSense is an extremely powerful and versatile solution to your advertising needs. Its reporting suite follows the same pattern; it is very extensive with access to a number of different dimensions for you to measure and improve the success of your AdSense units.

Fig 31.1 The top area of the reporting suite functions in a similar way to all the Google products we've reviewed so far. At the top right (just below your settings), you can adjust your date ranges and the area below allows you to export your report to either Excel (.csv – comma separated variables), a Google Drive spreadsheet, open in Google APIs Explorer or obtain 'BigQuery' code.

The left menu bar is split into three areas dealing with the whole account, the various channels that you make and the individual ad units on the page. Let's step through them one at a time.

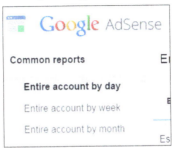

Fig 31.2 The first area is where you can see a broad overview of your account activity.

In the first set of reports, you can arrange your view by day, week or month to see the overall activity, including:

- number of pageviews
- number of clicks occurring on those pageviews
- CTR (Click Through Rate is clicks divided by impressions expressed as a percentage)
- CPC (Cost Per Click) for each click and an overall average
- RPM (Revenue per Mile) i.e. how much revenue you make per 1,000 page impressions

Fig 31.3 Note that here you can switch between day, week or month in the top right area of the graph, essentially doing the same thing as the left menu set allows.

A very handy feature here is the 'Add dimensions' drop-down menu (between the graph and the table on the left). This allows you to add the equivalent of a secondary dimension (as you did in Google Analytics) based on any of the left-hand menu sets.

Fig 31.4 With the addition of a secondary dimension, you can segment (slice and dice) your results in any way you wish.

Custom channel	Page views	Clicks	Page CTR	CPC	Page RPM ↓	Estimated earnings
VFX_and_CGI	549	2	0.36%			
3D_rendering	58	2	3.45%			
Houdini	44	1	2.27%			
df2 animationMaking	83	1	1.20%			

Fig 31.5 If I add the custom channels I created as my secondary dimension and then choose to order by 'Page RPM', I can see how my custom channels perform against each other over any time period. This will help me understand how best to distribute my channels over my blog. Here I've placed (via DFP) the AdSense custom channel 'VFX_ and_CGI' on higher traffic pages then the '3d_rendering' ad unit, which has a higher CTR engagement level. Advertisers buying AdWords campaigns using '3D rendering' are thus very precisely aligned with the content and most likely looking for specialised blogs to advertise on. They are also paying a premium to find blogs with a precisely defined audience. You too will see patterns in your traffic, engagement and CPC values that can help you raise your 'Page RPM' and ultimately your earnings.

The next set of menu items deals in more depth with your channels.

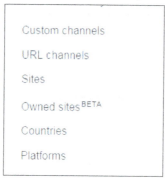

Fig 31.6 *The next menu set lets you go into more granular detail by pivoting your data around any of the items listed.*

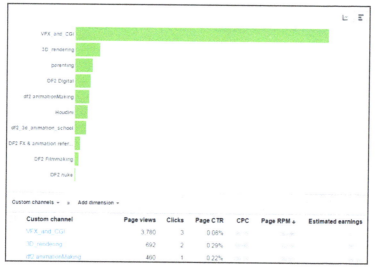

Fig 31.7 *You can now see the success (measured in terms of earnings) of the different custom channels you created. The great thing about this is that you can order the table according to any of the dimensions listed. Here the RPM on 'VFX_and_CGI' channel that I created is higher partly because it has had so many more pageviews than the other channels; being able to reorder my table by different dimensions (e.g 'page CTR') will normalise the figures to give me a better representation of how the channels perform relative to one another, rather than basing it purely on volume (which is the default way to view these figures).*

'URL channels' works in exactly the same way as 'Custom channels' do.

'Sites' also behaves in the same way, but orders them in terms of site variant names (e.g. if you have a Blogger account, the sites will divide up into country specific sites such as yourBlog.blogspot.co.nz, yourBlog.blogspot.ru and yourBlog.blogspot.ca).

'Owned Sites' will wrap all the variants into one, e.g. yourBlog. blogspot will show as one entry with all your other owned sites (yourBlog2.com and yourBlog3.info etc.).

Reporting on countries and platforms

The 'Countries' report, as you might expect, is an excellent way to arrange your metrics based on the country dimension.

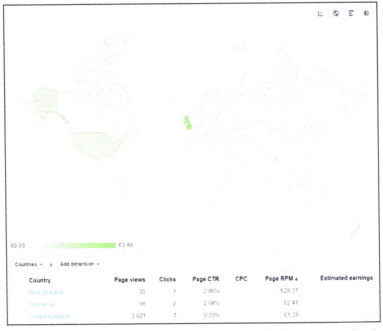

Fig 31.8 Clicking on any of the column headers will sort the data into ascending / descending order. This can help you to quickly identify which are your best-performing countries. You can add in extra dimensions by clicking on the 'Add dimension' drop-down to further segment your data.

'Platforms' will arrange the data in terms of the devices your ads are being viewed on.

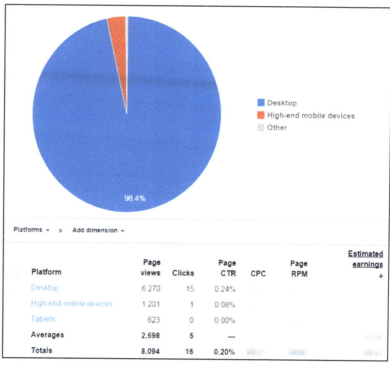

Fig 31.9 This works in the same manner as all the other reports and you can add a second dimension like 'Ad units' or 'Custom channel' to segment further and see exactly how your ad units are performing across all platforms. Compare and contrast this with the devices report in Google Analytics and you will gain valuable insight into how your blog layout can be optimised for mobile and tablet devices.

In the case of many responsive WordPress sites, this will help you to understand whether you have laid out your site in the best way to display your content and ads together. If you are getting high mobile traffic and you have a two-column blog layout, you'll notice that the second column is displayed below the first column on a mobile device. This means that the ads in your second column will not be visible on mobile devices (unless the visitor scrolls right the way down) and will account for why your advertising is not getting any user engagement on mobile devices. If this is the case, consider the layout of your blog and determine whether you can put ad units in the main content of the site instead.

Individual ad unit performance

The next menu set is all about the ads themselves and allows you to segment the attributes associated with the individual ads.

Ad units

Ad sizes

Creative sizes BETA

Ad types

Ad behaviour BETA

Ad networks

Targeting types

Bid types

Fig 31.10 Whereas the first two menu sets were about your account and audience, the third menu set focuses solely on the types of ad that are displaying on your blog.

Now if you've been following along, you know that I've been pushing for you to follow naming conventions for everything. Well your ad units are no exception; if you've named your ad units according to the sections on your blog(s), then these sets of reports will provide even greater insight. For starters, your 'Ad units' report will now tell you how each individual ad unit on each section of your blog has performed.

There are three distinct parts to the ad unit report, so let's look at them individually.

Export to Excel CSV ▾	Save report	Set as default report				Columns ▾
Estimated earn...	Ad requests	Coverage	Clicks	Ad request CTR	CPC	Ad request RPM
... ▾						

Fig 31.11 The top menu bar across the ad unit report lets you view the performance of whichever metric you are interested in.

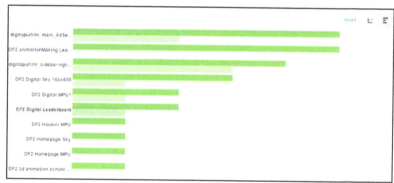

Fig 31.12 Again, the value of naming your ad units really comes through here because you can see which sections of your site are creating the most engagement. Combine this graph with any of the displays available in Fig 31.11 and you will really begin to understand how well the ads work for each section's audience. The light green bar is a comparison between the selected time period and the comparison time period, and you also have the option to view this as a line graph (top right corner).

Ad units » Add dimension ▾									
Ad unit		Ad requests ⓘ	Coverage	Clicks	Ad request CTR	CPC	Ad request RPM	Estimated earnings ◆
digitopiafilm_main_AdSense3_728x90_as	Edit	216	99.54%					
DF2 animationMaking Leaderboard	Edit	24	100.00%					
digitopiafilm_sidebar-right-1_AdSense1_160x600_as	Edit	213	100.00%					
DF2 Digital Sky 160x600	Edit	62	100.00%					
DF2 Digital MPU1	Edit	62	100.00%					
DF2 Digital Leaderboard	Edit	47	100.00%					
workingParent_general_sky	Edit	84	100.00%					
workingParent_general_MPU	Edit	82	100.00%					
DF2 animationMaking Sky	Edit	23	100.00%					
DF2 animationMaking MPU	Edit	23	100.00%					

Fig 31.13 No report anywhere in the Google ecosystem is complete without a tableful of details.

Briefly going back to the top area (Fig 31.11), you can switch between the metrics you wish to measure. In fact, this report goes beyond switching between them but actually allows you to plot them together on one chart.

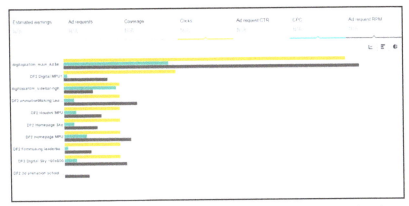

Fig 31.14 Selecting metrics at the top will add a different coloured bar — the colours are displayed below the name of the metric, i.e. the yellow line under 'Clicks', the 'green' line under 'CPC' and the purple line under 'Ad request RPM'. Coupled with a clear naming convention, this lets you quickly see the performance of your various ad units across different parts of your blog.

Note that you can switch between a line graph, bar chart or pie chart with the buttons in the top right corner.

The next unit will give you performance results solely for 'Ad sizes' so you can see what format of ad is gaining the most traction across any of the available metrics.

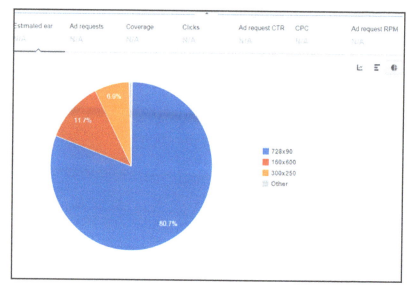

Fig 31.15 When you can see such a clear pattern, it may give rise to the thought of keeping only the Leader Board and dropping the other ad units – and have a second leader board at the foot of the article just above the share button – after all, a reader who has read through your whole article is clearly engaged enough to get to the end, and this type of visitor may be better primed to click on an ad at the bottom of the article. Remember that as the visitor scrolls down, he will lose the ads further up the page, so having ads lower down after the article may be a smart way to maintain engagement.

'Creative sizes' does the same thing as 'Ad sizes' but fills in any variation gaps for the different formats, e.g for the MPU it includes both the 300x250 and its variants the 250x250, the 336x280 and the 200x200. It's based on what AdSense could find at that particular instance to fulfil the advertising requirement.

'Ad types' does much the same thing except that we are dissecting according to the types of ads that display on your site, in terms of whether they are static image, animated image, text, rich media, Flash based ads and so on.

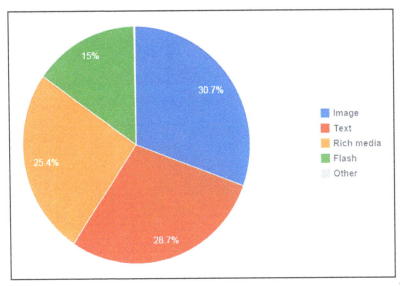

Fig 31.16 Sometimes the results of the 'Ad types' can be quite surprising, in this example, finding that 'Text' ads accounted for such a large proportion of the revenue. Sometimes bloggers think that they want only rich media ads on their sites and that there's no place for text ads (after all, they are a bit boring in comparison), but knowing the proportion of engagement that text ads build will avoid this mistake from happening. I do recommend running all the ad units for a few months so you can build up this data and find out what is working, before keeping what works and dropping what doesn't.

The 'Ad networks' list is about as close as you are going to get to seeing who has actually appeared on your blog. It applies the same metrics as you've seen elsewhere, but this time in relation to the ad network advertising that has appeared on your blog.

	Ad network
	Google AdWords
	AdRoll.com 3
	Quantcast
	Google: DCLK Bid Manager
	Criteo (UK)
	MediaMath
	Struq
	Rocket Fuel
	Google: Invite Media (Europe)
	Amazon.com (Europe)
	[X+1]

Fig 31.17 If you see one other (i.e. non-Google) network performing very strongly, it may be worthwhile exploring whether you can broker a better deal directly with that network because a strongly performing network clearly has advertisers that are meeting your audience's needs.

Finding out whether 'contextual' or 'interest-based' advertising works best on your blog

The 'Targeting types' is a very interesting report that shows how much delivery and engagement is happening across the 'Contextual' and the 'Interest-based' advertising being displayed. What you hope is that AdSense is delivering as much 'Contextual' advertising to your content as possible, but the way in which the real-time bidding occurs means that a lot of 'Interest-based' advertising is also being delivered. Here you are going to need to look at the two metrics together to understand how this distribution is working and whether it is successful.

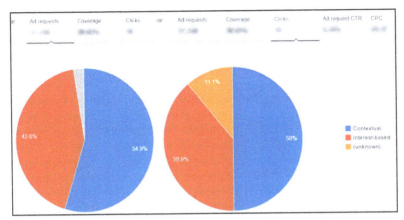

Fig 31.18 Here I've edited the diagram to show two pie charts together. On the left, you can see the distribution impression generated by choosing the 'Ad requests' metric at the top — how AdSense had distributed the advertising according to 'Contextual' (blue) and 'Interest-based' (red) metrics. On the right, I chose the 'Clicks' metric to see how my audience responded to the distribution that AdSense had served. Using this method, you will be able to see how well your content lends itself to AdSense 'Contextual' advertising and whether you get a better response from a 'Contextual' or 'Interest-based' approach.

The next item 'Bid Types' will break down your results according to the bid types that have been made on your blog, e.g. CPC (Cost per Click), CPM (Cost Per Mile) or CPE (Cost Per Engagement).

The final item in the list is a handy 'Events' button. What this does is to plot any of the major metrics with annotations on when you created or edited anything within your AdSense setup.

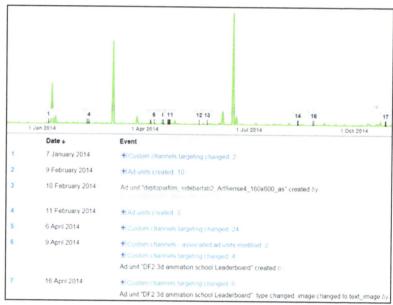

Fig 31.19 The 'Events' feature should show you what positive and negative changes you have made to increase engagement with your ads — as you start to optimise further, you'll soon see what works and what doesn't.

In this chapter, we've gone through the whole reporting section in AdSense, and you can now see how to measure your success with the way in which you choose to set the platform up. In fact, that brings an end to the section on ad networks/exchanges and AdSense in particular. We've now walked through the whole process of how you would set up, design, execute and measure the success of AdSense onto your site – other options are available too and they will work in a similar manner.

As you know, this whole book is about securing your own advertising deal and keeping that revenue, but I do think that there is a lot of value in using these types of exchanges/networks too, mostly because they are so quick to set up and monitor performance on.

Initially you may feel that these networks and exchanges will help plug gaps until you get to secure your own advertiser, but even when you do have your own deal you may still want to run these adverts alongside what you have negotiated. Bear in mind that the revenue you make through these sites will be subject to a number of people taking their cut. As a lot of this type of advertising is based upon actual clicks (CPC) or any acquisitions made through the click (CPA), your revenue will fluctuate; it's quite likely, in fact, to fluctuate below what you would make through your own deal. However, these platforms offer huge advantages too:

a) They will bring the advertisers to you – you do not need to chase advertisers and can get on with the important business of blogging.

b) They will target based both on 'Contextual' and 'Interest-based' – 'Interest-based' advertising is something no blogger is able to do on their own and as you will see from your own reports, delivering 'Interest-based' advertising based on the users' cookies can be incredibly powerful.

c) There is no advertising partner you need to satisfy through monthly reports and having to constantly justify their advertising spend with you.

Whichever way you decide to go, you are now armed with everything you need. Consider what you have learnt from the start of this book up to this point. You now understand Google Analytics, DFP and AdSense in great depth. With this knowledge you can now set out on a unique strategy that is as individual as your blog. Bear in mind what I said earlier – your blog will be forever growing and changing shape, you may start new blogs, you may go into joint ventures. The point is that whatever size and shape your blog takes, you now have all the tools and techniques at your fingertips to become very agile and very responsive. As well as being able to react quickly, you can now shape events and define where you want your blog to be.

Part 7:

In closing

Chapter 32:

Putting it all together with blogging.

So now we've come to the end of the book, I wanted to write a section about the whole process, step back from the software slightly and take a high-level view. This is where you will see the value of what you've learnt so far.

So where exactly have we journeyed?

We've gone through a lot of material, and we've done it all in great detail. The main premise of the book was to demonstrate the value of your blog to potential advertising partners and make an exchange of your advertising space for their advertising budgets using the three step WAB formula:

- Implement the analytics code – With the best will in the world, it will be hard to convince anyone to part with their advertising budget until you can at very least start to measure your traffic. Without this, how would you even know what your own traffic levels are?

- Analyse the data – This is the stage where you define your own KPIs and discover the value of your traffic. You can measure both the size and (just as importantly) the engagement of your audience. After all, it's the engagement that the advertiser is interested in, and using analytics you will be able to increase that engagement level.

- Refine and present this data to your advertising partners – Keep this maxim in mind: 'advertising spend follows audience'. The better you are able to present this to an advertiser, the easier it will to persuade them to part with their budget. In fact, when done correctly (which we've learnt how to do), there is often little persuading required, just a case of negotiating an amount (where you hold 'the balance of power' or know how to develop your blog to get yourself to hold 'the balance of power').

You then learnt how to deliver those advertisements, because after all the hard work of brokering a deal it would be pretty pointless if you weren't able to serve the adverts and report back on their performance. We went all the way through how to configure, implement and report on a free ad server (DFP), which will give you an incredible amount of flexibility when broking a deal, or indeed several deals.

In the section after that, you learnt about ad networks and exchanges with a focus on Google AdSense. Again we went through the entire configuration, implementation and reporting aspects to give you an in-depth understanding of the value that you can add to your blog from one of these setups.

So now it's time to pull all this together. You are, after all, a blogger and blogging is what you want to be doing more of. Well the good news is that the majority of the items you've gone through are a one-off setup cost; once you have your dashboards and alerts set up, the analytics and reports should come back to you and you can get on with the important business of blogging. But you will still need to keep returning to these three platforms. At first you will be coming back frequently, but as you gain more confidence you will return at pre-defined points in time, i.e. when you post a new blog post, when you make changes to your blog set up or when you want to measure the active engagement your social media channels bring back to your blog. There will be lots of events that you'd like to measure, so planning ahead for these events and knowing where to find the results will help you factor your analytics tasks into your blogging timetable.

Before setting yourself targets to achieve, find out where you are, find out what your best content is and create more of it, find out what your most active and engaged acquisition channels are and then use them to drive traffic to your blog. Define the different levels of engagement through these channels. Now you can start to make progress towards your target.

Speaking of those targets, your analytics will help you to define a 'roadmap' towards them. After installation, spend a few weeks just monitoring your traffic whilst continuing to blog as normal. This initial stage is about establishing the base level at which you are starting and will give you a realistic idea of how near or far from your target you are. If you are close to the target at the start, then ask yourself whether it's really a target. It may be too unambitious and would be better as a milestone towards a bigger goal.

Use this concept of milestones to mark out steps towards your target. For example, you may feel that you want to have a loyal readership generating 10,000 pageviews a month to be able to go directly to an advertiser. Here are the steps to achieve this:

- View your 'Pageviews' (under 'Audience | Overview') to see quickly how close to your target you currently are.

- View your new and returning visitors (under 'Audience | Overview') to establish currently what proportion of traffic comes back to your site.

- View the Pages/Session (also under 'Audience | Overview') to see how engaged your audience is with your content – the more pages they view, the more compelling the content.

- View the 'All Pages' report (under 'Behavior | Site Content') to find out which are your most popular pages.

- View the 'Channels' report to see where your traffic is coming from and how they behave once on your blog.

- Bundle all these up into a dashboard and you will very quickly see all this valuable data in one place. You can then make the right decision in super-fast time.

Monitor your dashboard as you start to make your on-site changes and work on your distribution methods. It's these distribution channels that you will want to make particular note of. *As we all know, we spend as much if not more time on distribution than we do on actual blogging,* so make sure that you use the UTM tagging functionality that we defined earlier (Chapter 17) and embed these into any shortened URL links you create. Set up 'Custom Alerts' (under 'Admin' | 'Personal Tools and Assets') to let you know when your daily or weekly target is reached (for the target of 10,000, you'd need a daily alert when you hit over 333 a day).

Now you have defined targets to measure your effort against. Without defining these parameters at the outset, you'd quite likely have no direction to ply your efforts against and be forever changing tactics, as you wouldn't know whether it was working or not. Defining these metrics gives you that clear target to aim towards and helps you plot milestones along the way. You will also know exactly how close to these milestones you are, what online activity is helping you get there and what activity is a waste of time. Try doing that without analytics.

Now factor in your time. This is an important concept. Many of us reading this book will have lofty ambitions of making blogging our full-time vocation, something that will pay us more than our day jobs do and ultimately allow us to gain a full-time income from. At the moment we may not be there, so we have limited time, what with all the other demands life makes of us. Therefore knowing what converts and what doesn't (and in what quantity they do or don't convert in), is very valuable for us so that we can make sure we spend our precious time wisely.

What works for one audience doesn't work for another and what conversion rates are good for one audience won't be appropriate for another. Use your analytics and collect your own data about your own audience. With this baseline in place, then you can start your own experiments and test your own hypotheses. Use a process of false positives (i.e. empirical testing to find out what doesn't work) to ultimately lead you to find out what does work. The analytics techniques that you have learnt in this book, coupled with knowing your audience, will get you there much quicker than you would expect. You will start to know what your audience likes, in which mediums they prefer to receive their content, how best to deliver your content to the right audience and how to grow your audience.

That's pretty valuable stuff, which will allow you to get on with what you love doing – blogging.

Chapter 33:

Where to go next.

So we've come to the end of the book. Now you are a web analytics savant, you can configure and serve any type of advertising on your blog and I am hoping you will soon see a substantial revenue stream.

Is that the end of your journey?

No, it's the start of your next journey.

As you progress through these journeys, remember and hold onto the purpose of your blog – the one you had when you first started. It's easy to get all excited about new technology, in whatever shape that comes, but unless you're blogging about analytics and digital technology, then the purpose of your blog is most likely to explore your passion and share it with like-minded people.

Now that you have one successful blog, you might be considering branching out and creating another, based on one of your other interests. This is achievable, but time and resources should definitely be budgeted carefully. I actually run several blogs and I have to tell you that giving enough time and attention to each blog is a real challenge. It's like having more than one child – all the blogs, like all the children, need your time and attention to thrive.

Keep in mind that each blog will have its own CMS (e.g. WordPress, Blogger, Tumblr) and its own social media accounts to manage. Fortunately though, the analytics and ad serving data will all be one place, so you now have a direct comparison between how your time and effort is divided across multiple blogs. Use the analytics that you've gathered to plan out your time between each of these. The analytics and ad serving data (in particular the AdSense reports, if you choose to tread that path) will put a monetary value on the advertising streams of each blog.

Let's finish off by talking about the money side of things. Monetisation will come with time. If your prime focus is on money, then blogging may not be the right thing for you. If you focus purely on monetising then you will miss your audience, and if you miss your audience, you will miss the money too. Keep writing, filming and recording audio for your audience. Use the analytics that we've put together here to deliver what your audience wants. If you are valuable to your audience and give them the things they need and want, then they will keep returning to you. If you can manage to grow your audience, then you will gradually begin to own that blogging space and monetisation will then naturally follow. You may be surprised to know that the monetisation of your blog will be less satisfying than the knowledge that you are helping people. Stay focused on helping people through your blog and monetisation will be a happy side effect.

Use the maxim, 'know-like-trust' when it comes to your sales process. Whatever it is that you are trying to sell, ask yourself, 'Will this bring real value to my audience and is it something that they want?' If the answer is genuinely, 'Yes,' then they will come to you and buy without you having to badger them. Badgering will lead them to mistrust you.

Think long-term. Whatever you are selling today has a shelf-life and you will have something new next year and the year after, whether it's a book, an online course or one-to-one consulting. It's a long game, so don't sacrifice your audience's trust and loyalty for a quick pay day. If you do, you'll be needing to find a new audience fairly soon, and we all know how time-consuming it is to build a new and trusting audience. Instead, build a long-lasting relationship with your audience, one which will bring more like-minded people to the party – people who will grow to know-like-trust you. Don't play with that trust.

Good luck with your adventures. I sincerely hope that you have gained a lot of value through this book. If you enjoyed reading it half as much as I enjoyed writing it, then we've both done very well. Do share your stories at my digital blog www.digitopiaDigital.com of how you used and applied this to your own blog and the results you've achieved from it.

If you did enjoy the book and found it valuable, please leave a review on the site where you purchased it from. Positive reviews are the lifeblood of successful authorship. Also do tell others who could benefit from the book about where they can purchase their own copy.

Thanks for reading and keep blogging!

All the best,

Farhan